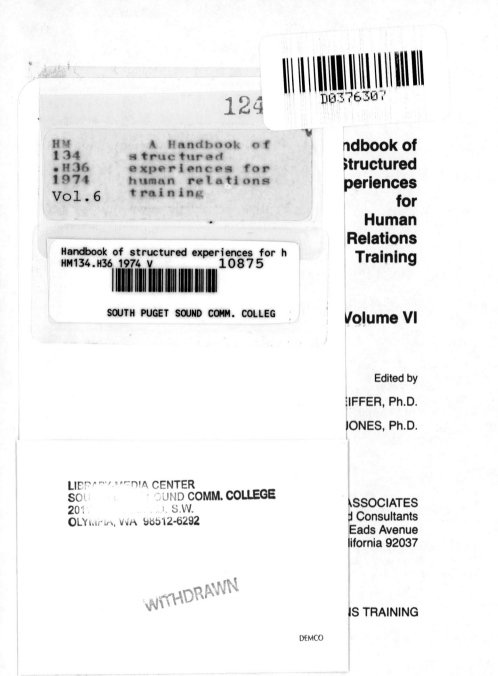

ndbook of
Structured
periences
for
Human
Relations
Training

Volume VI

Edited by

EIFFER, Ph.D.

JONES, Ph.D.

ASSOCIATES
d Consultants
Eads Avenue
lifornia 92037

S TRAINING

PREFACE

This volume of *A Handbook of Structured Experiences for Human Relations Training* continues the format and emphases of its five predecessors. The *Handbooks*, along with the *Annual Handbooks for Group Facilitators*, comprise the core of the Pfeiffer & Jones Series in Human Relations Training, which continues to be a clearing house for the emerging technology of this field.

Contributors to this volume vary widely in their backgrounds and professional affiliations. Of those twenty-seven individuals, ten are professors in various fields; eight identify themselves primarily as consultants; four are practicing psychologists; and five are training managers. The list includes persons in the fields of counseling, health education, education, organization behavior, psychology, commerce, speech, employee training, consultation, mental health, psychotherapy, staff development, program development, police training, and religion. Three contributors are women. Three contributors are from Canada and three are from Australia; the remainder work in the United States.

In this volume we have applied our accumulated experience to the editing process. We have selected and edited the pieces in accordance with these criteria: practicality, flexibility, workability, clarity, adaptability, and balance. We have taken liberties with some of the designs in order to make them more usable by the wide audience for which this book is intended.

The sharing that this series encourages is, we believe, beneficial to the development of the entire human relations training field, and we encourage group facilitators to submit their designs to us for possible inclusion in future publications. We suggest, in an effort to "demystify" this field, that professionals take advantage of one another's creative work.

This volume carries our unique copyright statement, and we urge our readers to study it carefully. It is gratifying to note that other publishers (although, unhappily, not the major ones) are beginning to use our reprint policy as a model.

We believe that this is the strongest volume of the *Handbooks* to date, and we are grateful to those who made it possible. A special note of recognition goes to Arlette Ballew, the production editor of this book, for her tireless patience with regard to details.

J. William Pfeiffer
John E. Jones

La Jolla, California
December, 1976

TABLE OF CONTENTS

*See Introduction, p. 2, for explanation of numbering.

INTRODUCTION

The activities included in this book were developed by group facilitators, and they have been selected because of their applicability to a wide array of education/training situations. They are named "structured experiences" in order to convey our belief that learning about human relations comes from examining direct interpersonal experiences. The *structure* is a designed series of interactions that produce the data for learning *(experience)* and a method of extracting useful insights.

Experience-based learning is facilitated by adherence to a model that begins with experience and ends with an answer to the question "So what?" The experiential model includes five cyclical steps:

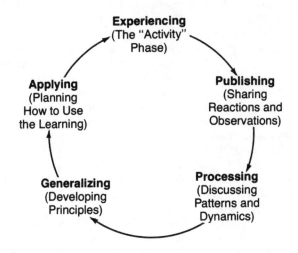

The *experiencing* phase involves some activity, such as fantasy, dyadic sharing, or group problem solving. If the model stopped at this point, however, training would be only "fun and games." Next, the participants engage in *publishing* their reactions to and observations of the activity. This is the data-generation phase; it leads logically into *processing*. It is our belief that processing is the key to the potency of structured experiences, and it is important that the facilitator allow sufficient time for this step. If the training is to transfer to the "real world," it is important to be able to extrapolate the experience from a laboratory setting to the outside world through *generalizing*. In this phase, participants develop principles, hypotheses, and generalizations that can be discussed in the final phase, *applying*. This final phase must not be left to chance;

facilitators need to ensure that participants wrestle with this practical considera-
tion. The actual application of behavior becomes new experience and begins the
cycle again.

There is no successful way to cut short this cycle. If structured experiences
are to be effective, the facilitator must supply adequate opportunities for
"talkthrough." The payoff comes when the participants learn *useful* things that
they take responsibility for applying.

These structured experiences are atheoretical in that they can be incorpo-
rated into education/training designs that have widely different theoretical content. They can easily be adapted to fit particular groups and organizational
realities—our suggestions for variations on each design are intended to facilitate
this process.

This collection brings the number of structured experiences that have been
published in the Pfeiffer & Jones Series in Human Relations Training to 220,
none of which are duplications.

Our published structured experiences are numbered consecutively
throughout the series of *Handbooks* and *Annuals*, in order of publication of the
volumes. A chart specifying the numbers of the structured experiences to be
found in each publication in the series and listing each structured experience
according to category is found at the end of this book. Although this categoriza-
tion is somewhat arbitrary, since any experience may be adapted for a variety of
uses, it will aid the facilitator in choosing an appropriate activity.

The six volumes of the *Handbooks* and their companion publications, the
Annual Handbooks for Group Facilitators (1972, 1973, 1974, 1975, 1976, and
1977), are fully indexed in the *Reference Guide to Handbooks and Annuals*
(Second Edition). The *Reference Guide* is an indispensable aid in locating a
particular structured experience, or a structured experience for a particular purpose, within the twelve books.

The twenty-four structured experiences in this volume are arranged according to the same principle used in the other *Handbooks* and in the *Annuals*; the
sequence is from simple to complex. The structured experiences at the beginning of the book can be conducted by almost anyone. The later activities carry
the potential to elicit significant emotional reaction in participants; therefore,
they require more experience and sophistication on the part of the facilitator
conducting them. This sequence, of course, represents our subjective judgment
of the complexity and possible volatility of the designs.

When selecting and adapting structured experiences, the facilitator should
take into account the following considerations: the learning needs of the participants, the goals of the training, the developmental level (readiness) of participants, and the facilitator's competencies. It bears repeating that the effectiveness of a structured experience primarily depends on adequate implementation
of the entire experiential model.

197. BEST FRIEND: A GETTING-ACQUAINTED ACTIVITY

Goals

I. To afford participants the opportunity to introduce themselves in a non-threatening manner.

II. To develop a climate for group interaction by sharing personal information.

Group Size

Any number of groups of eight to ten members each.

Time Required

Approximately forty-five minutes.

Materials

I. A Best Friend Introduction Sheet for each member.

II. A blank sheet of paper and a pencil for each member.

Physical Setting

An empty chair should be set in the center of the room.

Process

I. The facilitator briefly discusses the goals of the experience.

II. He instructs the group members to "identify in your own mind that one person outside this group who you think knows you better than anyone else—it may be your mother, father, wife, husband, brother, sister, or a close friend. We will call this person your 'best friend.'"

III. The facilitator distributes the Best Friend Introduction Sheets and pencils and tells the members to complete the sheets according to the instructions given. (Five to eight minutes.)

IV. Using the data from the Best Friend Introduction Sheet, each participant in turn is directed to stand behind the empty chair in the middle of the group and to introduce himself as he would expect his "best friend" to do it. Other information *not* on the sheet may also be added to the introduction. (Approximately two minutes each.)

V. During the introductions, other participants are encouraged to make note of information they might wish to pursue with each person being introduced. (Questions and comments are prohibited until all participants are introduced.)

VI. The facilitator leads a discussion of the experience, including relevant questions, comments, and feedback to the participants. The group members then discuss what they learned about themselves, and then about each other, as a result of the experience.

Variations

I. After step III, participants can be grouped in dyads to share the information on their Best Friend Introduction Sheets. They can be instructed to introduce each other to the entire group.

II. Participants can be encouraged to respond personally to the items on the Best Friend Introduction Sheet, i.e.:

"I am the kind of person who likes . . ."
"I very much appreciate and value . . ."
"Someday I would like to . . ."

III. After step III, the participants can tape their Best Friend Introduction Sheets to their chests and mill around silently, reading the sheets of other participants.

Similar Structured Experiences: *Vol. I:* Structured Experience 5; *Vol. II:* 42; *Vol. III:* 49; '73 *Annual:* 87, 88; *Vol. IV:* 101; '74 *Annual:* 125; '76 *Annual:* 173, 174; *Vol. VI:* 198.
Suggested Instruments: '74 *Annual:* "Self-Disclosure Questionnaire."

Submitted by Donald L. Garris.

Notes on the Use of "Best Friend":

BEST FRIEND INTRODUCTION SHEET

Instructions: Answer the following questions as you would expect your best friend (outside this group) to describe you.

I would like to introduce: _____

                                                              (name)

He/she is the kind of person who likes:

    1.

    2.

    3.

He/she greatly appreciates and values:

    1.

    2.

    3.

Some of his/her dislikes or pet peeves are:

    1.

    2.

    3.

Someday he/she would like to:

    1.

    2.

    3.

198. CHOOSE AN OBJECT: A GETTING-ACQUAINTED ACTIVITY

Goals

    I. To increase perception of oneself.

    II. To provide an opportunity to share personal perceptions.

    III. To provide an opportunity to receive feedback on perceived behavior.

Group Size

    Unlimited.

Time Required

    Approximately two hours.

Materials

    I. A collection of objects—at least twice as many objects as participants—of varying size, weight, composition, tactile sensation (roughness, smoothness, compressibility, etc.), and color.

    II. A container large enough to accommodate all the objects so that the participants may not see the objects.

Physical Setting

    A room in which the group members can be seated in a circle.

Process

    I. The facilitator briefly discusses the goals of the activity.

    II. He places the container full of objects in the center of the circle and gives the following directions:

        1. At the indicated time, the participants are simultaneously to move to the center of the circle and to select an object that they can identify with from those within the container.

        2. Each participant is to identify with a single object.

3. The participants are to examine as many of the objects as they can before selecting one.
4. The participants are to make their identification partially, at least, on the basis of color, texture, weight, size, and complexity of the object.

III. The facilitator instructs the participants to return to their original positions as soon as they have selected an object.

IV. As soon as all participants have returned to their positions, the facilitator indicates that participants are to explore their object and their identification with it. (Five minutes.)

V. He then directs participants to verbally share with the group their identification with their object. (The facilitator encourages the participants to speak in the first person, e.g., "I am rough in some places and smooth in others," in order to emphasize that the activity involves self-description rather than object description.)

VI. The facilitator directs the group members to give feedback to each other as to whether the projected identifications match or do not match their perceptions of each other.

VII. The facilitator then divides the participants into groups of three or four persons and indicates that they are to examine each other's objects and give to each other feedback on (1) similarities or dissimilarities with their own object images and (2) their own identification with the objects of others.

VIII. The observers report on their observations of the activity and the facilitator elicits observations from all members on the learnings gained from the experience.

Variations

I. Step VII can be eliminated.

II. More than one of each object can be included.

III. Objects can be traded within the group.

IV. Participants can be instructed to select an object while wearing blindfolds or with their eyes closed.

V. Participants can be sent outside to select their objects.

VI. In a community session, participants can select objects that represent how they see themselves in relation to the group.

Similar Structured Experiences: *Vol. I:* Structured Experience **19;** *Vol. III:* **49, 71, 72;** *'73 Annual:* **90;** *'76 Annual:* **181;** *Vol. VI:* **197.**

Suggested Instrument: *'76 Annual:* "Inventory of Self-Actualizing Characteristics (ISAC)."

Lecturette Sources: *'73 Annual:* "The Johari Window: A Model for Soliciting and Giving Feedback," "Risk-Taking"; *'75 Annual:* "Human Needs and Behavior."

Notes on the Use of "Choose an Object":

Submitted by Donald L. Thompson.

Structured Experience 198

199. T'AI CHI CHUAN: AN INTRODUCTION TO MOVEMENT AWARENESS

Goals

I. To increase body self-awareness.

II. To develop integrated, relaxed, economical, and balanced movement and activity.

III. To facilitate a feeling of "centeredness" in the here-and-now.

Group Size

Unlimited. The activity may be performed by one person or a large group.

Time Required

Approximately one hour.

Physical Setting

A room with a tile floor or low-pile rug on which the feet can pivot easily. A secluded outdoor place such as a woods or park is ideal. Indoors, about ten square feet per person is desirable.

Materials

A tape or record playing very slow, rhythmic, and soothing music.

Process

I. The facilitator begins by briefly describing t'ai chi and how it may be used:

T'ai Chi Chuan is an ancient Chinese discipline practiced for health, meditation, exercise, developing energy ("Chi") flow, and self-defense. The slow, flowing movements emphasize awareness and integration of the person: body awareness, breathing, relaxed and continuous movement, mental alertness and quietness, here-and-now, balance, and economy of movement.

Although there are classical forms that may take many years to learn, the *essence* of t'ai chi is the expression of oneself through integrated movement in everyday life.[1]

II. Participants are instructed to place themselves around the room, giving each other space for movement. The facilitator tells participants that they are to experiment with their bodies as he gives them directions. He suggests that participants attend to feeling and mood changes that occur during the process and to various areas of tension and overcompensation of balance during movement. He explains that "most of the time we ignore subtle bodily messages, uneconomical movements, and chronic muscle tensions by moving rapidly from where we are to where we want to go. We usually ignore or take for granted the in-between living, the *process* of moving."

III. The facilitator turns on the background music and goes through the T'ai Chi Chuan movements, pausing between each one as he instructs the participants:

1. Spread your feet about shoulder-width apart and parallel. Bend your knees slightly. Listen inwardly: feel the posture of your body, the slight strains and tensions . . . listen to your heartbeat . . . listen to your breathing.

2. Slowly, with your knees bent, let your pelvis tip up and forward until it is parallel with the floor. Now you can use your pelvis to cradle your stomach and intestines instead of holding them in with your diaphragm. Your diaphragm is used for breathing, not your chest. Let your shoulders relax, your chest relax, and let yourself breathe with your diaphragm, your lower abdomen. It just happens. Let yourself relax and breathe slowly and regularly.

3. Focus on your abdomen, about two inches below your navel. This is your *tant'ien*, your "center." Use your fantasy and imagine a large ball of fire or furnace there that will send streams of energy to any part of your body. Let yourself feel heavy or solid in your *tant'ien*.

4. With your *tant'ien* making you heavy below the waist, let the upper part of your body become light. Let your head float. Slowly let it roll around in smaller circles until you find the point where your head is balanced, face forward and chin slightly down. Imagine that the top of your head is held by a thin thread from the ceiling or sky. Between your abdomen "sinking" and your head "floating," your back will

---

[1]For a discussion of T'ai Chi Chuan, see Al Chung-liang Huang, *Embrace Tiger, Return to Mountain*. Moab, Utah: Real People Press, 1973.

become straight but not tight and rigid. Your back should always be perpendicular to the ground, otherwise you may "break posture" and lose balance or create unnecessary and distracting stresses.

5. Feel the rhythm of your breathing again and imagine waves of energy traversing your body with each breath.
6. Hold your tongue semi-rigid against the roof of your mouth (this affects the flow of energy).
7. Focus on your legs. Feel your weight distributed. In t'ai chi we deal with continually changing opposites: *Yin* and *Yang*—positive and negative, heavy and light, active and still, and so on. Let your weight shift from one leg to the other *very* slowly. The leg that carries the weight is your "heavy," "full," or *Yang* leg. As you shift your weight to the other leg it becomes "light," "empty," or *Yin*. All movements continually change from *Yin* to *Yang* and back again.

8. Keeping your legs bent and straight, step *very* slowly forward touching *heel first*. Let this be an "empty" step with no weight or energy shifting into the leg until it is completely flat on the ground. Continue slowly walking forward, heel first, then putting your foot down, then shifting your weight.
9. Now take a step backward, being careful not to "break posture." Touch backward first with your toes, again with an "empty" step until the foot is down, then shift the weight. Continue walking backward.

10. Now experiment, walking forward and backward and side to side, experiencing the shift in weight. Move slowly enough so that you can focus on the sensation and not on getting from one place to another. Imagine the energy from your *tant'ien* pouring from leg to leg and back again.
11. Just as your legs are opposites in t'ai chi, so too are your arms opposites of each other, and the upper part of your body is the opposite of the lower half. As you are moving, let one leg become heavy and the arm on the opposite side of your body become heavy. The other leg and opposing arm become light. As you move and your weight shifts, the opposing arms and legs also shift. Imagine again the energy moving from your *tant'ien* into your arms and legs.

12. We live in an ocean, a universe of energy. With each movement, imagine that you are swimming through that energy. Feel the movement of your body through that ocean. Let yourself completely relax, using only those muscles that are necessary for each movement. Let your arm movements be led by your hands. Imagine streams of energy emerging from the finger tips and palms.
13. When you follow your flow of energy, it moves you. All movement is circular, whether so large as to appear as a line or so small as to appear as a point.

14. Experiment with your movements. Use all parts of your body, all connected. Move up and down, forward and backward, side to side, inwardly and outwardly, withdrawing and expanding.

15. As you move again, become aware of your breathing. Let your breathing correspond with your movement. Exhale when moving down, back, or inwardly; inhale when moving up, forward, or expressively outward.

16. Use your peripheral vision and be open to all your senses. Do not focus on one thing and thereby limit yourself. Follow the flow of your sensory stimulation. Become aware of the synchrony of movement of your body and with others moving around you.

17. Imagine moving in the ocean of energy again. As someone else moves and creates a gap, fill it in with your own movement, as someone else fills the space you move from. Let all movements be as slow as possible with every person's movement complementing and filling in everyone else's movement. Everyone is connected by the same currents in the ocean of energy.

IV. Following the T'ai Chi Chuan movement instructions, participants are encouraged to experiment thoroughly with using the principles in everyday movements. The facilitator says that what they discover *then* is the essence of t'ai chi. He suggests that they try the movements for ten or fifteen minutes in the morning and the evening and during their day-to-day activities.

Variations

I. A brief form of the activity can be used as an energizer.

II. Another form of the martial arts or yoga can be substituted for the T'ai Chi Chuan movements.

III. The movement directions can be tape recorded.

Similar Structured Experiences: *Vol. II:* Structured Experience **47**; *'74 Annual:* **136.**

Lecturette Sources: *'75 Annual:* "Awareness Through Movement"; *'76 Annual:* "The Awareness Wheel," "Yin/Yang: A Perspective on Theories of Group Development"; *'77 Annual:* "Centering."

Submitted by David X. Swenson.

Notes on the Use of "T'ai Chi Chuan":

200. WORD-LETTER: A PROBLEM-SOLVING ACTIVITY

Goals

I. To demonstrate how problems are resolved when the alternatives are not clearly defined or the situation is ambiguous.

II. To explore group problem-solving processes.

Group Size

Twelve to twenty participants.

Time Required

Approximately one and one-half hours.

Materials

The following materials are to be compiled according to the Directions for Preparing Word-Letter Envelopes:

I. A large manila envelope.

II. Two smaller (letter-sized) envelopes that will fit inside the manila envelope.

III. An overall Word-Letter Instruction Sheet to be placed inside the manila envelope.

IV. A Letter Task Instruction Sheet and twenty-one 3″ x 5″ index cards, to be placed inside one of the letter-sized envelopes.

V. A Word Task Instruction Sheet and six 3″ x 5″ index cards, to be placed inside the other letter-sized envelope.

Physical Setting

Participants should be seated in a group-on-group arrangement so that the inner group has a table or floor space to work on and the outer group can see and hear the process clearly.

Process

I. The facilitator begins with a brief introduction, indicating that work groups often have tasks that are not well defined and that there is a process they go through to:
1. decide what the task is;
2. perform it; and
3. determine when it is completed.

II. Inner and outer groups are chosen so that the two groups are of about equal size, and the facilitator states that the groups will change positions when the first group has completed its task.

III. The outer group is told that it will observe the process used by the inner group and give feedback later on. Observation guides may be used, such as "What to Look for in Groups" ('72 *Annual*), "Process Observation Report Form (Volume I), or "Process Observer Recording Form" ('73 *Annual*).

IV. The facilitator then places the large envelope in the center of the work space and the group performs the task until it decides it is finished. The working group may ask the facilitator for further directions or clarification of the task. The facilitator responds by saying that the group must make this decision.

V. When the task has been completed, the facilitator initiates a discussion about the experience by asking about group and individual satisfaction with how the task was done. (Was everyone pleased with the outcome? Why or why not? Were minority opinions heard?) The facilitator also guides the group through the process by which it made its various decisions during the activity. (How was one task chosen over the other? What assumptions were made in choosing? Who led the group in deciding and working? How was the group's objective or target arrangement determined? Who was listened to and who was not? Who spoke and who did not?) Observations are then made by participants and observers.

VI. The two groups then reverse roles and positions so that the second (unopened envelope) task is done by those who had observed the first task.

VII. Step V is repeated.

VIII. Both groups then discuss the similarities and differences between the processes used by the two groups, and the facilitator leads the group in a discussion of how groups accomplish tasks.
Note: There are no "right" answers to these tasks.

Variations

    I. The same group can do both tasks.

    II. Two or more groups can do the task simultaneously and then share experiences.

    III. Observers can be directed to look for specific things in a group.

    IV. The activity can be performed by individual groups without the group-on-group arrangement.

    V. Another ambiguous task can be assigned.

Similar Structured Experiences: *Vol. I:* Structured Experiences **4, 7, 12;** *Vol. II:* **29, 31;** *'74 Annual:* **126.**

Lecturette Sources: *'72 Annual:* "Communication Modes: An Experiential Lecture"; *'73 Annual:* "Conditions Which Hinder Effective Communication"; *'76 Annual:* "Clarity of Expression in Interpersonal Communication"; *'77 Annual:* "Constructive Conflict in Discussions: Learning to Manage Disagreements Effectively."

Notes on the Use of "Word-Letter":

Submitted by Jordan P. Berliner.

Structured Experience 200

DIRECTIONS FOR PREPARING WORD-LETTER ENVELOPES

Inside a large (9" x 12" or larger) manila envelope, place two smaller envelopes and an instruction sheet stating:

> "This envelope contains two envelopes. One of the envelopes contains a letter task and the other a word task. Your task is to choose one of the two tasks and do it."

One of the two sealed envelopes is marked "Letter Task" and contains:

> Three 3" x 5" index cards marked A
> Three 3" x 5" index cards marked B
> Three 3" x 5" index cards marked C
> Three 3" x 5" index cards marked D
> Three 3" x 5" index cards marked E
> Three 3" x 5" index cards marked F
> Three 3" x 5" index cards marked G

and an instruction sheet stating:

> "This envelope contains cards on which letters of the alphabet have been printed. Your task is to arrange these cards."

The other sealed envelope is marked "Word Task" and contains:

> One 3" x 5" index card marked A
> One 3" x 5" index card marked BEST
> One 3" x 5" index card marked CAN
> One 3" x 5" index card marked DO
> One 3" x 5" index card marked EAGLE
> One 3" x 5" index card marked FAIRER

and an instruction sheet stating:

> "This envelope contains cards on which words have been printed. Your task is to arrange these cards."

All envelopes are to be sealed before they are given to the participants.

201. BREAD MAKING: AN INTEGRATING EXPERIENCE

Goals

I. To experience collaborating on an unusual group task.

II. To focus on the sensory, fantasy, and creative aspects of food preparation.

III. To provide a sensory, nonverbal background for integrating learning in the final stages of a workshop.

Group Size

An unlimited number of triads.

Time Required

Approximately one hour and twenty minutes (one sixty-minute period followed by one twenty-minute period later on).

Materials

I. Ingredients and utensils appropriate for bread making.

II. Copies of a bread-making recipe for each triad.

Physical Setting

A room large enough so that all triads can work separately and a kitchen with ovens that can accommodate all the loaves made.

Process

I. The facilitator discusses the goals of the activity and briefly outlines the process to be experienced. He invites the participants to consider the sensory and playful aspects of making bread.

II. The participants are formed into triads (groups of three) and copies of a bread-making recipe are distributed.

III. The facilitator announces that the bread-making activity is nonverbal and directs the triads to begin. (During the times when the triads are not actively involved in the task, the facilitator assigns appropriate discussion topics.)

19

IV. After the loaves are baked, the members sample their bread and share it with others.

V. If the structured experience is not conducted as a closure activity, the facilitator leads a group discussion of the process.

Variations

I. Several recipes can be presented on one sheet (or a number of bread-making recipe books can be made available) so that the members of each triad can select the recipe that represents them. They can also vary the recipe and the shape of the loaf to represent or suit themselves.

II. The bread-making materials can be organized by committees.

III. The triads can be instructed to form on a particular basis, e.g., participants I want to be with, participants whom I perceive to be similar to me, etc.

IV. The total group can process the experience.

Similar Structured Experiences: *Vol. I:* Structured Experience **23**; *'72 Annual:* **86**; Vol. IV: **114.**
Lecturette Source: *'75 Annual:* "Re-Entry."

Notes on the Use of "Bread Making":

Submitted by Anthony G. Banet, Jr.

202. DOMINOES: A COMMUNICATION EXPERIMENT

Goals

I. To enhance awareness of factors that help or hinder effective interpersonal communication.

II. To explore the effect on task-oriented behavior of shared versus unshared responsibility.

Group Size

An unlimited number of groups of four members each.

Time Required

Approximately one and one-half hours.

Materials

I. Two matching sets of three dominoes each for each four-person group. The number of boxes of dominoes needed can be computed from the chart below.

Boxes of Dominoes	Maximum Number of Groups	Unused Dominoes
2	9	2
4	18	4
6	28	0

II. Newsprint and a felt-tipped marker.

Physical Setting

A room large enough for the groups to work without disturbing each other. There should be chairs available for all participants and lapboards for half the members of each group.

Process

I. The facilitator introduces the activity. He divides the participants into groups of four members each and instructs the members of each group to name themselves A, B, C, and D.

II. The facilitator directs the members of each group to seat themselves so that A and B are sitting back to back and C and D are sitting where they can watch A and B.

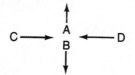

He announces that members A and B will be engaged in a task while members C and D will observe them.

III. A and B from each group are each given one of the matched sets of three dominoes, which they may compare. They also receive lapboards.

IV. The facilitator conducts round 1 (unshared responsibility):
1. A is instructed to make a design with his dominoes on his lapboard. Once it is made, he is not to change it.
2. C and D are to observe A and B, paying special attention to what helps and what hinders effective communication.
3. A instructs B on how to make a design identical to his own.
4. B, C, and D may not talk or communicate in any way with each other or with A.
5. After A has given what seem to him to be adequate instructions to B, he may turn and compare his design with that of B.
6. C and D give brief feedback to A and B.
7. All participants rotate, repeating the activity until each has had a turn giving directions.

V. The facilitator leads a brief discussion of what has happened during round 1, listing on newsprint those observed behaviors that helped or hindered communication. He also leads a discussion on the effects of unshared responsibility on task accomplishment.

VI. The facilitator conducts round 2 (unshared responsibility):
1. A is instructed to make a design, as before.
2. C and D are observers, as before.
3. After A indicates that he is ready with a design, B asks him questions in order to make his replication of A's design.
4. The facilitator directs A to answer B with only a "yes" or "no" response.

5. He adds that C and D may not talk or communicate with either A or B.
6. When B decides that he has completed his task, he may compare his design with A's.
7. C and D give brief feedback, as before.
8. All participants rotate to each position, as before.

VII. The facilitator leads a brief discussion, as before; he *adds to* the list begun at the end of round 1 and elicits comments from the participants on the effects of unshared responsibility, as they experienced it during round 2.

VIII. The facilitator conducts round 3 (shared responsibility):
1. A makes a design, as in rounds 1 and 2.
2. C and D observe, as in rounds 1 and 2.
3. A and B are instructed that they may talk freely as B attempts to duplicate A's design.
4. C and D observe, but do not communicate with A or B.
5. When A and B think that they have completed the task, they may each check the other's design.
6. C and D give feedback, as before.
7. All participants rotate to each position, as before.

IX. The facilitator adds to the list of behaviors that helped or hindered communication, as in step VII. The group discusses the effects of shared responsibility on task accomplishment and contrasts round 3 with rounds 1 and 2.

X. The facilitator then leads the total group in a discussion of the experience, pointing out or eliciting similarities to real-life situations. (It is often helpful to give a lecturette here on task and maintenance functions in a problem-solving setting, using as examples behaviors listed during the three rounds.)

Note: The groups will finish their tasks at different speeds. The facilitator can suggest that members who care to "practice" for the next round may do so until all have finished.

Variations

I. Tinkertoys, children's blocks, etc., can be used instead of dominoes, or the participants can draw designs (see *Volume I*, Structured Experience 4).

II. The activity can be carried out by triads, with only one person observing.

III. The rotation process can be eliminated to shorten the time.

Structured Experience 202

IV. The quartets can write one or two generalizations about each round after
its completion. These can be in the form of open-ended sentences, such
as:

> One-way communication . . .
> Unshared responsibility . . .
> Communication rules . . .
> Two-way communication . . . .

Similar Structured Experience: *Vol. I:* Structured Experience **4.**

Suggested Instrument: *'74 Annual:* "Interpersonal Communication Inventory."

Lecturette Series: *'73 Annual:* "Conditions Which Hinder Effective Communication"; *'74 Annual:* "Five Components Contributing to Effective Interpersonal Communications," "'Don't You Think That . . . ?': An Experiential Lecture on Indirect and Direct Communication."

Notes on the Use of "Dominoes":

Submitted by Stephan H. Putnam. Adapted from an activity included in *The Human Communications Training Manual for Air Force Populations*, edited by Sterling Gerber, Ph.D., revised 1973.

203. HEADBANDS: GROUP ROLE EXPECTATIONS

Goals

I. To experience the pressures of role expectations.

II. To demonstrate the effects of role expectations on individual behavior in a group.

III. To explore the effects of role pressures on total group performance.

Group Size

Ten to fifteen members. In a large group, a small group performs while the remaining members observe.

Time Required

Approximately forty-five minutes.

Materials

One headband for each participant. The headbands can be made of heavy paper or 5" x 7" cards with 10" strings attached to the ends of the cards (so that the cards can be tied around the heads of the participants). Each headband is lettered with a felt-tipped marker to show a particular role and an explanatory instruction as to how other members should respond to the role. Examples:

Comedian: Laugh at me.
Expert: Ask my advice.
Important Person: Defer to me.
Stupid: Sneer at me.
Insignificant: Ignore me.
Loser: Pity me.
Boss: Obey me!
Helpless: Support me.

Physical Setting

A circle of chairs—one for each participant—is placed in the center of the room.

Process

I. The facilitator selects ten to fifteen volunteers to demonstrate the effects of role pressure.

II. He places a headband on each member in such a way that the member cannot read his own label, but the other members can see it easily.

III. The facilitator provides a topic for discussion and instructs each member to interact with the others in a way that is natural for him. Each is cautioned not to role play but to be himself. The facilitator further instructs the group to react to each member who speaks by following the instructions on the speaker's headband. He emphasizes that they are not to tell each other what their headbands say, but simply to react to them.

IV. After about twenty minutes, the facilitator halts the activity and directs each member to guess what his headband says and then take it off and read it.

V. The facilitator then initiates a discussion, including any members who observed the activity. Possible questions are:
1. What were some of the problems of trying to "be yourself" under conditions of group role pressure?
2. How did it feel to be consistently misinterpreted by the group, e.g., to have them laugh when you were trying to be serious, or to have them ignore you when you were trying to make a point?
3. Did you find yourself changing your behavior in reaction to the group's treatment of you, e.g., withdrawing when they ignored you, acting confident when they treated you with respect, giving orders when they deferred to you?

Variations

I. The activity can be adapted by using role descriptions appropriate for the participants, for example: black, teacher, nurse, policeman, parent, etc.

II. One headband can be left blank to demonstrate the power of inference or projection.

III. The activity can be preceded or followed by a lecturette about role theory, symbolic interaction, or living up to others' expectations.

Similar Structured Experiences: *Vol. I:* Structured Experience 9; *Vol. II:* **38;** *Vol. III:* **56;** *'75 Annual:* **138;** *Vol. V:* **171;** *'76 Annual:* **174, 184;** *Vol. VI:* **214.**
Lecturette Source: *'76 Annual:* "Role Functions in a Group."

Notes on the Use of "Headbands":

Submitted by Evelyn Sieburg. The origin of the activity is not known.

Structured Experience 203

204. MOTIVATION: A SUPERVISORY-SKILL ACTIVITY

Goals

I. To demonstrate the value of goal setting for task achievement.

II. To demonstrate the positive role of a supervisor in developing the motivation to achieve.

Group Size

An unlimited number of dyads.

Time Required

Approximately one hour.

Materials

I. A dart board and three darts for each dyad.

II. A Motivation Score Sheet for each participant.

Physical Setting

A room large enough for the dyads to throw darts simultaneously.

Process

I. The facilitator describes the goals of the experience.

II. Participants are told to form pairs. They are encouraged to select a partner with whom they feel they will work well.

III. The dyads are instructed to decide which member will first be the "employee" and which will be the "supervisor." They are informed that one round consists of three dart throws by the employee and that after four rounds they will reverse roles.

IV. The Motivation Score Sheets and darts are distributed to participants. Employees take one practice round (throw three darts each) and their supervisors record their scores in turn. The employees are informed that they will need to declare their goal (what their score will be) before playing the next round.

V. Employees and supervisors are instructed that they are to negotiate the goal for each round before the employee takes the shots.

VI. During the activity, the supervisor records the goals and the achieved scores for each round. The facilitator observes the motivating and performing behaviors of the participants.

VII. After the fourth round, the employees and supervisors reverse roles. The new employees now complete a practice round and four more rounds, setting goals and keeping score, as before.

VIII. When all participants have completed four rounds, the facilitator processes the experience. He may focus the discussion on the motivating behaviors of the supervisors, the quality of the contract between employee and supervisor, and the feelings of the employees as they were performing.

IX. After the discussion is complete, employees and supervisors work through another three rounds each. Supervisors are encouraged to actively motivate their employees to perform better.

X. Another discussion at the conclusion of these rounds focuses on supervisory skills: the effects of feedback on performance, collaborative planning of strategy, and positive aspects of contract setting.

Variations

I. The experience can be used to demonstrate the effects of positive reinforcement by having all participants cheer the employee or, alternatively, to illustrate negative reinforcement, degrade his performance.

II. Other simple games—making paper airplanes, memorizing the sequence of a set of playing cards, etc.—can be substituted for the darts and dart board.

III. The first four rounds can be conducted without setting goals.

IV. The activity can be carried out by triads, with the third person serving as scorekeeper-observer.

Similar Structured Experiences: *Vol. II:* Structured Experience **45**; *'73 Annual:* **100**; *Vol. VI:* **210**.

Suggested Instrument: *'72 Annual:* "Supervisory Attitudes: The X-Y Scale."

Structured Experience 204

Lecturette Sources: *'72 Annual:* "Assumptions About the Nature of Man," "McGregor's Theory X-Theory Y Model," "The Maslow Need Hierarchy," "Criterion of Effective Goal-Setting: The SPIRO Model"; *'74 Annual:* "The 'Shouldist' Manager"; *'75 Annual:* "Human Needs and Behavior."

Notes on the Use of "Motivation":

Submitted by Ken Frey and J. David Jackson.

MOTIVATION SCORE SHEET

Employee_____

Round	Goal	Actual Score	Round Total
Practice			
1			
2			
3			
4			

(Discussion)

5			
6			
7			

Structured Experience 204

205. CIRCLE IN THE SQUARE:
A COOPERATION/COMPETITION ACTIVITY

Goals

 I. To demonstrate how cooperation and competition can affect winning and losing.

 II. To explore how winning and losing are defined, perceived, and measured.

Group Size

An unlimited even number of groups of two to eight members each.

Time Required

Approximately one hour.

Materials

 I. Two felt-tipped markers of different colors for each pair of groups.

 II. One sheet of newsprint, with the chart with thirty-six squares drawn on it, for each pair of groups.

 III. A watch with a second hand.

Physical Setting

One room large enough to accommodate the activity.

Process

 I. The facilitator explains to the participants that they will have an opportunity to invest ten cents each in order to gain a greater return on their money. He emphasizes the fact that skill is all that is required to achieve this success. He then collects ten cents from each of the participants.

 II. The facilitator displays on newsprint a chart with thirty-six squares.

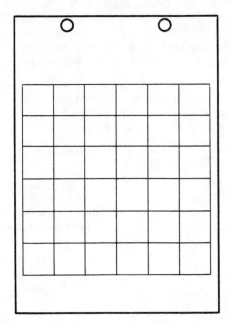

He explains that the activity will be carried out by pairs of groups, using the chart and felt-tipped markers. (The facilitator does not use the word "teams" or introduce the element of competition in his description of the activity.) He explains that the activity will be carried out as follows:

1. Each group will use a different-colored marker to place a circle in a square during the group's "move." Each group's objective is to complete rows (horizontal, vertical, or diagonal) of five squares marked with circles of the group's color.
2. A group will mark one circle in one square per move, and moves will be made alternately by the two groups.
3. Each group is allowed thirty seconds for each move; the move is lost if not made within that time.
4. Each group will be allowed ten minutes for a strategy session before the marking begins.
5. The activity will be completed when each group has had an opportunity to make fifteen moves.
6. The return on the members' investment is based on the number of rows of five consecutive squares filled in by their group. (No mark can be counted twice.)

Structured Experience 205

III. The facilitator divides the participants into pairs of groups. Each group meets separately for ten minutes to plan its strategy. Each group elects a "marker" who will draw a circle in the group's chosen square on the newsprint. The "marker" can confer with his group before each move but must stay within the time limit of thirty seconds per move.

IV. The facilitator flips a coin to determine which group in each pair will move first. The groups then move alternately until each group has had a chance to move fifteen times. The facilitator keeps the groups within the thirty-second time period for each move.

V. At the completion of the activity, the facilitator "scores" the activity according to the following chart:

Players Per Group	Return/Line Completed (3 Lines Maximum)
2-3 people	$ .10-.15
4-5 people	.15-.20
6-7 people	.25-.30
8 people	.35

He then pays the groups the return on their investments according to the chart. Any remaining money is distributed to the members of the "winning" group.

VI. The facilitator leads the participants in a discussion of the experience, focusing on the following elements:

1. The meaning of winning. (Is it winning money, making the other group lose, achieving a higher score than the other group, gaining cooperation from the other group, etc.?)
2. The feeling of winning. (This can be explored in terms of winning money, achieving more points, preventing the other group from winning, etc.)
3. The fact that the facilitator did not verbally try to create a competitive atmosphere.
4. The fact that most groups are so competitive they do not see that if they cooperate and do not block the other group's moves, each group can complete three lines (a win-win solution). In the process of competing, most groups will block the other group's moves to the extent that neither may complete any lines at all.
5. The concepts of cooperative and competitive achievement, win-win versus win-lose strategies, trust, etc. (These can be discussed and related to the group's experience.)

Variations

    I. Other tasks for the groups can include words to be formed from selected letters, with points for the number of words and letters.

    II. Instead of using different-colored markers, paired groups can mark their squares with different symbols.

    III. The payoff schedule can be adapted to reflect the completion of rows of three, four, five, or six squares.

    IV. At the end of round 8, each group can choose either to confer among themselves or to confer with the members of their paired group. (Ten minutes.)

    V. The structured experience can be carried out without using money.

    VI. The total group can decide before the activity how any remaining money will be spent or distributed or the group can make this decision after the activity, making sure that it is a win-win solution.

Similar Structured Experiences: *Vol. II:* Structured Experiences **32, 33, 36;** *Vol. III:* **61;** *Vol. V:* **150, 164;** *'76 Annual:* **179;** *'77 Annual:* **189, 194;** *Vol. VI:* **210, 218.**

Lecturette Sources: *'72 Annual:* "Assumptions About the Nature of Man," "McGregor's Theory X-Theory Y Model"; *'73 Annual:* "Win/Lose Situations."

Notes on the Use of "Circle in the Square":

_____
Submitted by Clyde E. Lee.

Structured Experience 205

206. SUBMISSION/AGGRESSION/ASSERTION: NONVERBAL COMPONENTS

Goals

I. To experience and differentiate the nonverbal components of assertive behavior from those of aggressive and submissive (nonassertive) behavior.

II. To increase awareness of one's own assertive behavior.

Group Size

Ten to fifty participants.

Time Required

Approximately thirty minutes to one hour.

Materials

Newsprint and a felt-tipped marker.

Physical Setting

A room large enough for individuals to move about freely without restricting the space of others.

Process

I. The facilitator asks participants to call out their associations to the word "assertiveness" and records their responses on newsprint.

II. The facilitator tells each participant to think of the most *submissive* (nonassertive) individual he has ever seen and to imagine the behavioral characteristics he associates with that person. The facilitator then directs the participants to mill around, each acting out nonverbal submissive behavior.

III. After five minutes, he directs the participants to "freeze" in a fixed position depicting submissive behavior, to look around at the other people, and to identify the similarities in their behavior.

IV. The facilitator elicits comments about the nonverbal manifestations of submissiveness (or nonassertiveness). He lists these on newsprint. (Usually the comments will include the behavioral components of eye contact, body posture, facial expression, and interaction distance.)

V. After all responses are recorded by the facilitator, participants are directed to change from submissiveness to aggressiveness. Again, they are told to think of the behavior of the most *aggressive* individual they have ever encountered and to use the room in any way they want in order to role play the aggressive behavior nonverbally. The only stipulation is that there be no physical abuse or destruction of property.

VI. At the end of five minutes, the facilitator instructs the participants to remain in a "frozen" position depicting aggressive behavior and to look around the room and observe similarities in the behavior of the other members.

VII. The facilitator then elicits comments about the similarities of the observable nonverbal behaviors that are related to aggressiveness and records the comments on newsprint.

VIII. The facilitator describes the behavioral characteristics of an *assertive* person, focusing on the nonverbal components of assertive behavior. ("The assertive person establishes good eye contact and stands comfortably but firmly on two feet with his hands loose at his sides. The assertive person stands up for his rights while respecting the rights of others, is aware of his feelings and deals with them as they occur, manages his tensions and keeps them within a constructive range." He may add, "The assertive person makes 'I' statements, uses cooperative words, makes empathic statements of interest, and seeks a balance of power.")

IX. The facilitator directs the participants to think of a person they have observed who seems to fit best the description of an assertive person and to depict that person's behavior nonverbally.

X. After five minutes, the facilitator directs the participants to "freeze" as before and to observe and compare each other's behavior.

XI. The facilitator leads a discussion on the differences between submissive, aggressive, and assertive behavior and lists these on newsprint. He may compare this listing to the original responses to the word "assertiveness" elicited in step I.

XII. The facilitator leads the group members in a discussion of the application of assertive behavior in everyday situations. Participants are encouraged to

Structured Experience 206

discuss situations in which they are usually assertive and ones in which they might wish to become more assertive.

Variations

I. If the group is large, part of the group can participate in the nonverbal exercise, while the remainder can be process observers.

II. Participants can be verbal while being submissive, aggressive, and assertive, and these components can be processed as well.

Similar Structured Experiences: *Vol. I:* Structured Experience 22; *Vol. II:* **44;** *Vol. III:* **72;** '75 *Annual:* **138.**
Lecturette Source: '76 *Annual:* "Assertion Theory."

Notes on the use of "Submission/Aggression/Assertion":

Submitted by Gerald N. Weiskott and Mary E. Sparks.

207. STAFF MEETING: A LEADERSHIP ROLE PLAY

Goals

I. To illustrate various styles of leadership and patterns of accommodation.

II. To explore the effects of the interaction of leadership style and pattern of accommodation on individual motivation and decision making.

Group Size

Three to six groups of four to seven members each.

Time Required

Approximately two and one-half hours. Additional time is required if lecturettes are to be presented.

Materials

I. One Staff Meeting Information Sheet for each participant.

II. For each work group, one Staff Meeting Role Sheet (principal roles) for one of the following: Mr./Ms. Trask, Mr./Ms. Purpull, or Mr./Ms. Wyant.

III. One or two Staff Meeting Role Sheets each for Mr./Ms. Upshaw, Mr./Ms. Indoff, and Mr./Ms. Ambrose (teacher roles) for each work group.

IV. One copy of the Staff Meeting Instructions for Principals Sheet for each work group.

V. Three to six Staff Meeting Instructions for Teachers Sheets for each work group.

VI. One Staff Meeting Topics Sheet for each work group.

VII. Three Staff Meeting Reaction Sheets for each participant.

VIII. One Staff Meeting Principal's Decision Sheet for each work group.

IX. Three to six Staff Meeting Teacher's Decision Sheets for each work group.

X. One Staff Meeting Predicted and Actual Results Sheet for each participant and each work group. (If there are more than three teachers in a group, *two* sheets for each group are required.)

XI. One 5″ x 8″ index card for each participant.

XII. A felt-tipped marker for each work group.

XIII. Newsprint.

Physical Setting

A room large enough to accommodate role playing and discussion. Additional rooms may be used for the group role-playing sessions ("staff meetings").

Process

I. The facilitator introduces the technique of role playing and describes the forthcoming role play as an exploration of organizational behavior in schools.

II. The facilitator forms work groups or asks participants to form themselves into work groups of four to seven members each.

III. He distributes copies of the Staff Meeting Information Sheet and answers any questions.

IV. The facilitator appoints a "principal" for each work group or asks each work group to appoint one. The remaining work group members are "teachers."

V. The facilitator distributes one of the three Staff Meeting "principal" Role Sheets to each principal, being sure that at least one copy of each different principal role is distributed. He then distributes "teacher" roles to the remaining group members, being sure that at least one of each of the three different teacher roles is distributed in each group.

VI. The facilitator distributes cards and markers and asks each participant to make a name card indicating his role name and title. If two of the same teacher roles are distributed in a work group, an "A" or "B" should be placed in parentheses in front of the teachers' names to distinguish between the two, i.e., Mr. (A) Upshaw; Mr. (B) Upshaw.

VII. The facilitator distributes copies of the Staff Meeting Instructions for Principals Sheet and the Staff Meeting Instructions for Teachers Sheet to appropriate participants.

VIII. The participants take a few minutes to study their roles and instructions individually. The facilitator answers any questions.

IX. The facilitator distributes copies of the Staff Meeting Topics Sheet to each principal. The principal then conducts staff meeting #1. (Five to ten minutes.)

X. At the end of the staff meeting, the facilitator distributes a copy of the Staff Meeting Reaction Sheet to each participant. Participants complete these sheets individually.

XI. Steps IX and X are repeated for staff meetings #2 and #3.

XII. The facilitator announces that it is now almost the end of the school year and that he has a memo for each principal and teacher from the office of the superintendent of schools. He then distributes copies of the Staff Meeting Principal's Decision Sheet and the Staff Meeting Teacher's Decision Sheet to the appropriate participants, who complete them individually.

XIII. The facilitator distributes copies of the Staff Meeting Predicted and Actual Results Sheet to the participants and to each group. Each group makes a compilation of its members' decisions on the extra copy of the Staff Meeting Predicted and Actual Results Sheet and gives the composite sheet to the facilitator.

XIV. The facilitator displays all group's results on newsprint and conducts a general discussion of the role-playing experience, focusing on the goals of the activity.

Variations

I. Groups can be formed in various ways based on known leadership or accommodation patterns of participants.

II. Principals can be rotated to different work groups after each of the first two staff meetings to enable all teachers to experience different leadership styles. If this variation is employed, the discussion at the end of the role play focuses on teachers' reactions to the three different leadership approaches rather than on the tenure and transfer decisions.

III. The background situation and role descriptions can be rewritten to suit the backgrounds or needs of the group.

IV. The facilitator can present a lecturette on the theories underlying the role descriptions.[1]

---

[1]See R. R. Blake and J. S. Mouton, *The Managerial Grid* (Houston, Texas: Gulf, 1964); D. M. McGregor, *The Human Side of Enterprise* (New York: McGraw-Hill, 1960); R. P. Moser, "The Leadership Patterns of School Superintendents and School Principals," *Administrator's Notebook*, September 1957, 6, 1-4; and R. Presthus, *The Organizational Society* (New York: Alfred A. Knopf, 1962).

Structured Experience 207

Role Description	Grid Style (Blake)	Leadership Style (Moser)	Assumptions (McGregor)	Accommodation Patterns (Presthus)
Trask	9,1	Nomothetic	Theory X	
Purpull	1,9	Ideographic	Theory X	
Wyant	9,9	Transactional	Theory Y	
Upshaw				Upward Mobile
Indoff				Indifferent
Ambrose				Ambivalent

Similar Structured Experiences: *'72 Annual:* Structured Experience **80**; *'73 Annual:* **98**; *'74 Annual:* **133, 134, 135**; *Vol. V:* **158**; *'75 Annual:* **139**; *'76 Annual:* **178**; *'77 Annual:* **193**.

Suggested Instruments: *Vol. I:* "T-P Leadership Questionnaire"; *'72 Annual:* "Supervisory Attitudes: The X-Y Scale," "Intervention Style Survey"; *'73 Annual:* "LEAD Questionnaire"; *'74 Annual:* "S-C Teaching Inventory"; *'76 Annual:* "Leader Effectiveness and Adaptability Description (LEAD)."

Lecturette Sources: *'73 Annual:* "Conditions Which Hinder Effective Communication"; *'74 Annual:* "Hidden Agendas"; *'76 Annual:* "Leadership as Persuasion and Adaptation"; *'77 Annual:* "A Practical Leadership Paradigm."

Notes on the Use of "Staff Meeting":

Submitted by Ernest M. Schuttenberg.

STAFF MEETING INFORMATION SHEET

Union Junior High School is one of the two junior high schools in a suburb of a large manufacturing city. There are nearly nine hundred students at Union and thirty-three teachers, 61 percent of whom are tenured teachers. A principal, assistant principal, two guidance counselors, a secretary, and two clerks make up the office staff.

The school has a good academic reputation, and efforts are being made to meet the continually changing needs of the student body. The school building is twenty-five years old, and the school is organized departmentally with each teacher working individually in a self-contained classroom.

School policies and regulations for staff and students are well defined and available in writing in teacher and student handbooks. This is the principal's sixth year at the school. While problems arise from time to time, the situation at Union Junior High School seems to be stable and under control.

STAFF MEETING ROLE SHEET

Mr./Ms. Trask, Principal

You are the principal of Union Junior High School. You have been a school administrator for ten years, and this is your sixth year as principal at this school.

You have been successful as a school administrator because you are task centered. You have always stressed to your teachers that the job of educating children is a difficult and demanding one and that all staff members need to exert constant effort to achieve educational goals.

As a result, while not all teachers consider you their friend, most of them respect you and comply with your wishes when you make requests of them.

It has been your experience that most teachers do not like to take on any more responsibility than they have to and that they prefer to have the principal provide the leadership. Also, you have found most teachers to be rather lazy and resistant to change. As a result, you have discovered that "coming on strong" and insisting that teachers follow your directions produce favorable results in most cases. After all, you are getting paid to make things happen at your school, and teachers need to realize this.

STAFF MEETING ROLE SHEET

Mr./Ms. Purpull, Principal

You are the principal of Union Junior High School. You have been a school administrator for ten years, and this is your sixth year as principal at this school.

You have been successful as a school administrator because you are person centered. It is very important to you that teachers be satisfied and happy in their work. You have always made an effort to protect your teachers from the some-times unreasonable demands made on their time by parents or by the office of the superintendent.

As a result, teachers consider you their friend, and most of them make a real effort to comply when you occasionally ask them to do something extra around school.

It has been your experience that most teachers do not like to take on any more responsibility than they have to and that they prefer to have the principal provide the leadership. You are willing to do this, but you rely on gentle persuasion rather than direct orders. After all, it is more important to have a satisfied staff of teachers than to have all your requests carried out.

STAFF MEETING ROLE SHEET

Mr./Ms. Wyant, Principal

You are the principal of Union Junior High School. You have been a school administrator for ten years, and this is your sixth year as principal of this school.

You have been successful as a school administrator because you are both task centered and person centered. You recognize that teachers have individual needs and goals and that schools have organizational needs and goals. As you work with teachers, you have always tried to find where these two sets of needs and goals intersect and thus to gain the commitment of teachers to the quest for educational excellence.

As a result, teachers regard you as fair and personally interested in them and in the school. You make every effort to involve teachers meaningfully in planning, implementing, and evaluating various aspects of the school program.

It has been your experience that most teachers are willing to assume responsibility and to work diligently to attain results to which they are committed. After all, if teachers are a part of the planning and decision-making process, they will take pride and satisfaction in striving to achieve school goals.

STAFF MEETING ROLE SHEET

Mr./Ms. Upshaw, Teacher

You are a nontenured teacher at Union Junior High School. Before coming to this school you taught for two years in an adjacent state. This is your second year at Union Junior High.

You have found teaching to be a very rewarding profession. Education is the most important process in life, and you are proud to be part of an institution that helps young people shape their lives. While classroom situations are sometimes difficult, you pride yourself on your dedication to your duties as an educator.

You have maintained good relationships with all the school administrators with whom you have come in contact. After all, administrators have difficult jobs and tough decisions to make. Since you hope to become a principal some day, you are quite willing to go along with most administrative requests, even if you do not totally agree with some of them.

In short, you like teaching because of the future career opportunities it affords.

Structured Experience 207

STAFF MEETING ROLE SHEET

Mr./Ms. Indoff, Teacher

You are a nontenured teacher at Union Junior High School. Before coming to this school, you taught for two years in an adjacent state. This is your second year at Union Junior High.

You have found teaching to be a pretty good job, as jobs go. Of course, it is sometimes difficult to put up with the nonsense of the kids in class, but you have developed a way of putting on a gruff exterior which keeps them in line most of the time. Otherwise, there are no problems.

With regard to the administration, you do just enough around school so as not to arouse the adverse attention of the principal. You would prefer to take on as few extra assignments as possible, especially those that might result in additional work in the evenings or over the weekends. Evenings and weekends are the only times you can really enjoy life: participating in sports, being active socially, and pursuing your hobbies.

In short, you like teaching because of the free time it gives you off the job.

STAFF MEETING ROLE SHEET

Mr./Ms. Ambrose, Teacher

You are a nontenured teacher at Union Junior High School. Before coming to this school, you taught for two years in an adjacent state. This is your second year at Union Junior High.

You have mixed feelings about teaching from your experience to date. On the one hand, you get a great deal of satisfaction from working with students, helping them learn and grow. Then, too, there are the professional status and intellectual stimulation you enjoy with colleagues who share the same educational mission.

On the other hand, you dislike the arbitrary use of power and authority often displayed by the school administration. On a number of occasions you have witnessed decisions made in the principal's office that you knew were not in the best interest of kids. And you do not feel that your life is entirely your own since you must often comply with administrative decisions that were made without consulting you.

In short, you like teaching but dislike schools.

STAFF MEETING INSTRUCTIONS FOR PRINCIPALS SHEET

You are to conduct three five- to ten-minute staff meetings with a small number of the nontenured teachers on your staff at Union Junior High. The purpose of each meeting is to discuss a particular problem with the teachers and to enlist their aid in dealing with it.

The approach you take in each staff meeting should be consistent with your administrative values and experience as described in your role sheet.

After each of the three staff meetings, you will be asked to make a brief written record of any decisions reached, your reactions to the meeting, and your feelings about the teachers with whom you met.

For the purposes of this activity, it will be assumed that there is approximately a month between each meeting. The meetings, therefore, are not particularly related in content, even though you will be meeting with the same group of teachers each time.

STAFF MEETING INSTRUCTIONS FOR TEACHERS SHEET

You will be asked to attend three five- to ten-minute staff meetings to be conducted by your principal at Union Junior High. The principal will inform you of the purposes of each meeting.

The approach you take in conducting yourself at each staff meeting should be consistent with your values, desires, and experiences as described in your role sheet.

After each of the three staff meetings, you will be asked to make a brief written record of any decisions reached, your reactions to the meeting, and your feelings about the principal and other teachers.

For the purposes of this activity, it will be assumed that there is approximately a month between each meeting. The meetings, therefore, are not particularly related in content even though you and the same group of teachers will be meeting with the principal each time.

Structured Experience 207

STAFF MEETING TOPICS SHEET

Staff Meeting #1:

Student behavior has been getting a bit out of hand in the cafeteria lately. You think that it would help the situation if an additional faculty member would serve on cafeteria duty during each of the three lunch periods to assist the two teachers already on duty. Meet with your teachers to discuss this problem and seek a solution.

Staff Meeting #2:

Student discipline in the classroom has become a problem, judging from the number of office referrals over the last month. You think that a special faculty study committee on this subject would serve a useful function. Meet with your teachers to discuss their service on such a special committee.

Staff Meeting #3:

The Union PTA has recommended that improved communications be fostered between parents and teachers. You feel that a program of home visitations by teachers would be a help. Meet with your teachers to discuss this problem and their part in helping to solve it.

STAFF MEETING REACTION SHEET

My "name" is: Meeting Number:

_____   1   2   3
(write in)   (circle one)

Take a few minutes to jot down your reactions to the meeting just completed:

1. Decisions reached or outcome of the meeting:

2. Your reactions to the meeting:

3. Your feelings about others in the meeting:

STAFF MEETING PRINCIPAL'S DECISION SHEET

My "name" is:

_____

(write in)

It is now near the end of the school year. The superintendent's office has asked you to provide a recommendation regarding tenure for each of the nontenured teachers in your building.

Based on what you know about the teachers you have been meeting with over the past three months, please recommend each of them by checking the appropriate box on the form below for each teacher.

Be guided in your decision only by your value system and assessment of their potential as educators in this school system. Recommend only those teachers from the list whom you actually met with:

RECOMMENDATIONS FOR TENURE	(Check one box for each teacher you met with.)					
	A. Upshaw	A. Ambrose	A. Indoff	B. Upshaw	B. Ambrose	B. Indoff
1. Recommend Unequivocally						
2. Recommend, but with Reservations						
3. Do not Recommend						

STAFF MEETING TEACHER'S DECISION SHEET

My principal's "name" is: My "name" is:

_____   _____

(write in)   (write in)

It is now near the end of the school year. The superintendent's office has asked you to make a decision regarding transferring to the other junior high school next year or staying at Union.

Based on your experience at Union Junior High this year, and especially on the meetings you have had with your principal, please indicate your decision by checking the appropriate box on the form below.

For the purposes of this activity, please assume that your decision will be held in strictest confidence by the office of the superintendent and that your wishes will be honored. Be guided in your decision by your value system and the extent of your desire to work at Union Junior High again next year:

OPTIONS	MY DECISION (Check one box)
1. Definitely want to stay at Union Junior High	
2. Will stay, but with reservations	
3. Request a transfer from Union	

Structured Experience 207

STAFF MEETING PREDICTED AND ACTUAL RESULTS SHEET

Use the matrices below to record with stroke counts (‖‖ |||) the actual decisions reached by participants in the role play. Asterisks (*) indicate those decisions predicted on theoretical bases.

PRINCIPALS

Trask, Principal	Ambrose	Indoff	Upshaw
1. Recommend Unequivocally			*
2. Recommend, but with Reservations	*		
3. Do not Recommend	*	*	

Purpull, Principal	Ambrose	Indoff	Upshaw
1. Recommend Unequivocally	*	*	*
2. Recommend, but with Reservations	*	*	
3. Do not Recommend			

Wyant, Principal	Ambrose	Indoff	Upshaw
1. Recommend Unequivocally	*		*
2. Recommend, but with Reservations	*		*
3. Do not Recommend		*	

TEACHERS

Ambrose, Teacher	Trask	Purpull	Wyant
1. Definitely Stay			*
2. Stay, but with Reservations			*
3. Request Transfer	*	*	

Indoff, Teacher	Trask	Purpull	Wyant
1. Definitely Stay		*	
2. Stay, but with Reservations			*
3. Request Transfer	*		

Upshaw, Teacher	Trask	Purpull	Wyant
1. Definitely Stay		*	*
2. Stay, but with Reservations	*	*	
3. Request Transfer			

Structured Experience 207

208. TEAM DEVELOPMENT: A TORI MODEL

Goals

I. To study TORI growth processes.

II. To practice applying a theoretical model to group self-diagnosis.

Group Size

Unlimited.

Time Required

Approximately two and one-half hours.

Materials

I. Blank paper and a pencil for each participant.

II. Newsprint, felt-tipped markers, and masking tape (optional).

Process

I. The facilitator announces the goals of the experience and summarizes the process. He tells the participants that they will study the TORI model by examining its individual parts and then putting them together in the context of task-group functioning.

II. The facilitator divides the participants into four subgroups and distributes paper and pencils to them. He says that each group will create a model of an ideal task group with regard to one of the four TORI growth processes: trust, openness, realization, and interdependence. He assigns one dimension to each group. (If there are more than about twenty-four participants, they may be divided into eight groups, so that each dimension will be explored by two groups simultaneously.) The facilitator instructs the groups that they will each give a five-minute presentation of their model to the rest of the members. He encourages them to be creative in developing their presentation and says that they may use role play, simulation, or any media or props that will effectively communicate their model.

III. The facilitator briefly explains the four concepts of TORI to the members. (He may list these on newsprint so that the members can refer to them later.) A brief summary of the four TORI factors is as follows:

1. Trust: interpersonal confidence and absence of fear.
2. Openness: free flow of information, ideas, perceptions, and feelings.
3. Realization: self-determination, being role free, doing what you want to do.
4. Interdependence: reciprocal influence, shared responsibility, and leadership.

IV. The groups formulate their models and prepare their presentations. (Thirty minutes.)

V. The facilitator instructs the groups to diagnose the way they functioned as work groups in terms of the TORI dimension they have discussed and to prepare to report on this diagnosis. (Ten minutes.)

VI. Each group is called on to present its model and to report on its own functioning in terms of the model. (Five minutes each.)

VII. When all presentations have been made, the facilitator directs the members of each group to discuss the integration of the four TORI concepts within a task group and to formulate three or four statements (generalizations) that depict the interrelationships between the four dimensions of the TORI model. (Twenty minutes.)

VIII. Each group is then called on to report its statements to the rest of the participants.

IX. The facilitator leads the total group in a discussion of the TORI model.

Variations

I. Other models of human interaction may be used.

II. Members may be assigned to the task groups to serve as process consultants.

III. Each subgroup may select the particular TORI dimension it will explore.

Similar Structured Experiences: *Vol. III:* Structured Experience **55;** *Vol. IV:* **118;** *Vol. V:* **166, 171;** *'77 Annual:* **196;** *Vol. VI:* **216.**

Suggested Instruments: *Vol. III:* "Group-Climate Inventory"; *'76 Annual:* "Leader Effectiveness and Adaptability Description (LEAD)"; *'77 Annual:* "TORI Group Self-Diagnosis Scale."

Structured Experience 208

Lecturette Sources: *'72 Annual:* "TORI Theory and Practice"; *'73 Annual:* A Model of Group Development"; *'74 Annual:* "Cog's Ladder: A Model of Group Development."

Notes on the Use of "Team Development":

Submitted by Gary R. Gemmill.

209. INTROSPECTION: PERSONAL EVALUATION AND FEEDBACK

Goal

To provide an opportunity for participants to compare their self-assessment with those of others.

Group Size

Any number of groups of five to seven participants each.

Time Required

Approximately forty-five minutes.

Materials

I. An Introspection Work Sheet and a pencil for each participant.

II. Newsprint and a felt-tipped marker.

Physical Setting

One room large enough to accommodate the groups, with a writing surface for each participant.

Process

I. The facilitator introduces the activity as a way to help participants look at their attitudes and feelings about themselves in relation to the way other people describe themselves. He encourages the participants to be honest in their responses.

II. The facilitator distributes pencils and copies of the Introspection Work Sheet to participants and directs them to find a place in the room where they can mark their work sheets in relative privacy. He instructs the participants to initial or otherwise code their work sheets on the back so that they can be identified later on.

III. The facilitator answers any questions and then tells the participants to begin marking their work sheets.

IV. When most participants have completed their task, the facilitator gives a one-minute warning. At the end of that time, he collects the work sheets. He divides the participants into groups of five to seven members each and randomly distributes—on the floor or table in the middle of each group—one completed work sheet for each group member. (Participants do not get their own work sheets.)

V. Participants look over the work sheets in their groups and exchange observations, reactions, etc., among themselves. The facilitator advises the groups to record any patterns or observations on each work sheet. (A line may be drawn between the X's on each work sheet, thus illustrating any patterns.)

VI. The facilitator again collects the work sheets and places them on a table, face down. The participants are instructed to retrieve their own work sheets (identifying them by the initial or code on the back of each sheet) and to read the comments made on their work sheets by other participants. (Ten minutes.)

VII. The total group is reassembled. The facilitator solicits the members' reactions to the notes made on their work sheets. He then goes through the work sheet items, directing participants to indicate their own responses to each item by raising their hands. From this, he illustrates the group norms on newsprint.

VIII. Subgroups report on their findings and discussions. The facilitator leads the members in a discussion of the learnings gained from the experience.

Variations

I. Each participant may receive an additional work sheet, on which he writes his name and which he gives to another person, asking that person to complete it in terms of how that person sees him. Each member then compares his personal work sheet with the one completed by another member and discusses his reactions to the similarities and differences with the members of his small group. Members are asked to describe why they think their descriptions of themselves are different from (or similar to) other people's descriptions of them.

II. Participants can discuss their own work sheets rather than those of others.

III. The group members can develop the adjectives to be used on the work sheets.

IV. A semantic differential[1] may be used on the work sheet, and the results may be computed in terms of Osgood, Suci, and Tannenbaum's clusters: activity, potency, and evaluative dimensions.

Similar Structured Experiences: *Vol. V:* Structured Experience **168;** *'76 Annual:* **174, 180;** *Vol. VI:* **197.**

Suggested Instrument: *'74 Annual:* "Self-Disclosure Questionnaire."

Notes on the Use of "Introspection":

Submitted by Dennie L. Smith.

[1]This structured experience is a variation of the classic semantic-differential technique (Charles E. Osgood, George J. Suci, & Percy H. Tannenbaum, *The Measurement of Meaning*. University of Illinois Press, 1967).

INTROSPECTION WORK SHEET

The following words were selected to enable you to record your perceptions of yourself. You are to indicate these by placing an "X" on one of the spaces between each pair of words. The distance from the "X" to a word indicates the degree to which it represents your view of yourself.

I AM

Impulsive ___: ___: ___: ___: ___: ___: ___: ___:	Cautious
Relaxed ___: ___: ___: ___: ___: ___: ___: ___:	Tense
Interesting ___: ___: ___: ___: ___: ___: ___: ___:	Boring
Self-Confident ___: ___: ___: ___: ___: ___: ___: ___:	Timid
Insecure ___: ___: ___: ___: ___: ___: ___: ___:	Secure
Modest ___: ___: ___: ___: ___: ___: ___: ___:	Arrogant
Pleasant ___: ___: ___: ___: ___: ___: ___: ___:	Unpleasant
Mature ___: ___: ___: ___: ___: ___: ___: ___:	Immature
Agreeable ___: ___: ___: ___: ___: ___: ___: ___:	Disagreeable
Friendly ___: ___: ___: ___: ___: ___: ___: ___:	Unfriendly
Attentive ___: ___: ___: ___: ___: ___: ___: ___:	Inattentive
Compassionate ___: ___: ___: ___: ___: ___: ___: ___:	Malicious
Competent ___: ___: ___: ___: ___: ___: ___: ___:	Incompetent
Compulsive ___: ___: ___: ___: ___: ___: ___: ___:	Flexible
Industrious ___: ___: ___: ___: ___: ___: ___: ___:	Lazy
Happy ___: ___: ___: ___: ___: ___: ___: ___:	Sad

210. DARTS: COMPETITION AND MOTIVATION

Goals

   I. To develop awareness of the factors involved in motivation.

  II. To increase awareness of the effects of motivation/incentives on the attitudes and performance of a given task in an intergroup competitive situation.

Group Size

Between twelve and twenty participants divided into groups of three to four members each.

Time Required

Approximately one and one-half hours.

Materials

   I. A dart board (cork board with a hand-drawn target area 2½" in diameter can be substituted for a dart board) for each group.

  II. Five darts for each group.

 III. A Darts Score Sheet and a pencil for each group.

  IV. A tape measure.

   V. Masking tape.

  VI. "Prizes" for one member and one group. (These need not be material objects.)

 VII. Newsprint and a felt-tipped marker (optional).

VIII. A stopwatch (optional).

Physical Setting

Participants are seated in a "U" or circular pattern in a large room. The corner areas of the room should be set up for the activity prior to the session as follows:

1. Targets are mounted to the wall. The height of the targets should be relative to the average height of the participants. Groups should be separated by as much distance as possible.
2. Distances of 9', 10', 11', 12', and 13' are measured from the bases of each wall on which the targets are mounted. These spots are marked by applying masking tape to the floor at the respective distances and labeling each tape accordingly.

Process

I. After explaining the goals of the activity, the facilitator defines the task: each member is to score as many "hits" as possible in *each* of three rounds. A "hit" is hitting the target area on a board with a dart so that the dart remains in the designated area for at least a few seconds. The facilitator demonstrates, showing the designated area (on a standard dart board, the *two* innermost circles are the target area). He continues with the following instructions:

1. Each participant will be allowed seven practice throws immediately before he begins his round. During practice and the first round, participants are to stand *behind* the line closest to the target. (This line is marked 9'.)
2. Each round will consist of twenty-five throws for each participant. Those individuals not performing the task (throwing darts) are responsible for keeping score of the number of hits and total throws on the Darts Score Sheet and for handing darts back to the thrower.
3. When each person's score is recorded, the entire group will be given the instructions for round 2.

II. The facilitator forms groups of three or four members each and distributes the Darts Score Sheet, a pencil, and darts to each group. He answers any questions.

III. Round 1 is conducted.

IV. The facilitator explains that based on the distribution of hits in round 1, a handicap will be assigned to each participant for round 2, on the following basis:

Number of Hits in Round 1	Distance for Round 2
10 or less	9'
11-13	10'
14-16	11'
17-19	12'
20 or more	13'

Handicaps are assigned, and the facilitator instructs each participant to record his handicap on the Darts Score Sheet on the line marked "X."

V. The facilitator instructs participants to conduct round 2 just as they did round 1, i.e., practice, rules, recording, etc., using their handicap lines as the distance from which the darts are thrown.

VI. After all scores have been recorded for round 2, the facilitator points out that, because of the handicaps, the scores should be approximately equal. The groups discuss this point.

VII. The facilitator announces that in round 3 the same procedure will be used as for round 2 and that prizes will be awarded for the outstanding single score and highest average group score (ties to be run off).

VIII. Round 3 is conducted. If there are any ties, runoffs are held to determine the winners.

IX. The facilitator announces the highest individual score and highest group score and awards the incentive prizes.

X. The members discuss the experience in their subgroups. Suggested questions are:

1. What was the effect of the incentives on the performances of individuals and groups? What other motivational factors were present?
2. How did competition affect your performance? If you realized that you were not going to earn a prize, what feelings did you have? What effect did this have on your performance? What was the effect of posting scores?
3. Would your performance have been any different within a different subgroup? Why?
4. What observations can you make about each other's behavior during the rounds? Compare round 1 to round 3.
5. What were your feelings regarding the standards that were established (handicaps, rules)?
6. Were any other standards imposed on the task either by the subgroup or by yourself?
7. *For managerial or supervisory personnel:* How does what you have experienced here apply to the everyday situation you face in motivating your subordinates, especially in terms of incentives versus needs, competition, rules, attitudes toward performance, productivity, boredom and fatigue, and discipline?

XI. The total group is then reconvened and the facilitator leads the participants in processing the experience.

Structured Experience 210

Variations

I. Rounds can be shortened.

II. Time standards of three and one-half to four minutes can be imposed for each round.

III. After each round, groups can be instructed to discuss their outcomes and dynamics.

IV. In subgroups of four, one individual can be assigned to observe the interaction that takes place during each round and report back to the reconvened group at the end of the session.

V. Money can be collected from all participants to provide the prize.

VI. The total group can determine the nature of the prizes, e.g., a place of honor at dinner, a special treat, etc.

VII. Other types of "darts" made of Velcro®, magnetic material, etc., may be used.

VIII. "Pitching pennies" into circles or squares on the floor may be substituted for dart throwing.

Similar Structured Experiences: *Vol. II:* Structured Experience **36;** *Vol. III:* **54;** *'72 Annual:* **78;** *'73 Annual:* **100;** *Vol. IV:* **105;** *Vol. V:* **160, 161;** *Vol. VI:* **204, 218.**

Lecturette Sources: *'72 Annual:* "Assumptions About the Nature of Man," "McGregor's Theory X-Theory Y Model," "The Maslow Need Hierarchy," "Criteria of Effective Goal-Setting: The SPIRO Model"; *'74 Annual:* "The 'Shouldist' Manager."

Notes on the Use of "Darts":

Submitted by Samuel Dolinsky.

DARTS SCORE SHEET

	Group Members			
Round **1.**				
X.	( )	( )	( )	( )
2.				
3.				

Group Average

_____

211. HELPCO: AN OD ROLE PLAY

Goals

I. To study the processes of organization development (OD) consultation.

II. To develop OD diagnosis, consultation, and observation skills.

III. To compare the relative effectiveness of two or more forms of group leadership in competing work teams.

Group Size

A minimum of seventeen participants (eighteen to twenty-four is ideal).

Time Required

Approximately three hours.

Materials

I. Blank paper and a pencil for each participant.

II. One 3" x 5" index card with a different role description from the Participant Role-Description Sheet for each member of the management systems firm and for each representative of the First Town Bank.

III. A Management Systems Firm Background Sheet for each member of the architectural firm and for the observer of that group.

IV. A Management Systems Firm Instruction Sheet for each member of the architectural firm and for the observer of that group.

V. A Client Instruction Sheet for each member representing the First Town Bank and for the observer of that group.

VI. A HELPCO Consultant Instruction Sheet for each member of the HELPCO team and for the observer of that group.

VII. Newsprint and a felt-tipped marker (optional).

Physical Setting

A room large enough for several teams to work without distracting each other.

Process

I. The facilitator introduces the activity as an organization development intervention involving a management systems firm; its client, the First Town Bank; and an OD consulting firm, HELPCO.

II. The facilitator selects three volunteer participants to be the consultants from HELPCO, three participants to be the representatives of the First Town Bank, and three participants to serve as process observers. The remaining participants are designated as members of the management firm and are divided into a minimum of two design teams (preferably of three members each—a team leader and two designers) and the president and vice president of the management firm. If there are more than seventeen participants in the group, a member is designated as the manager of the management firm; any others are assigned to design teams.

III. The facilitator distributes blank paper and a pencil to each participant. He then distributes a different management systems firm role-description card, a copy of the Management Systems Firm Background Sheet, and a copy of the Management Systems Firm Instruction Sheet to each member of the management firm. He gives a different First Town Bank role-description card and a copy of the Client Instruction Sheet to each representative of the First Town Bank. He gives a HELPCO Consultant Instruction Sheet to each member of the HELPCO team. He allows ten minutes for the participants to study their materials.

IV. During the ten minutes, the facilitator meets with the observers separately. He assigns one the task of observing the members of the management firm and gives him a copy each of the Management Systems Firm Background and Instruction Sheets. He assigns the second observer the task of observing the representatives of the First Town Bank and gives him a copy of the Client Instruction Sheet. The third observer is instructed to observe the members of HELPCO and receives a copy of the HELPCO Consultant Instruction Sheet. The facilitator emphasizes that the observers are to report on the organizational functioning of the three observed groups, management and communication within the groups, group processes and group dynamics, and the consultation processes between groups. The facilitator then instructs the observers to plan how they will observe and the method they will use to report their observations.

V. The facilitator instructs the participants to begin the activity by having the bank representatives contact the president of the management firm, describe their objectives, and ask for a proposed design for a training program in problem solving for management. (Fifteen minutes.)

Structured Experience 211

VI. The members of the management firm decide how the proposal is to be handled and give instructions to the design teams. (Ten minutes.) During steps V and VI, the members of HELPCO are instructed to observe the interactions between members of the other groups.

VII. Each management design team formulates a proposal for a training program in problem solving for management personnel. (Twenty minutes.) While the management teams are conferring, the client (bank) representatives develop the criteria they will use in reacting to the program proposal.

VIII. The management firm decides which proposal to present to the client. (Ten minutes.)

IX. If they have not done so by now, the management firm members call in the HELPCO team. (This may be done at any time in steps V through VIII and can take up to twenty minutes.)

X. The management firm presents its proposal to the bank representatives. At the same time, the HELPCO team reviews by itself what it has learned from working with the management firm and formulates a consultation strategy. (Ten minutes.)

XI. The bank representatives meet with members of the management firm and critique the proposed training program (based on the criteria they have formulated) giving comments, suggestions, etc., and asking for a new— and final— proposal. (Five minutes.)

XII. The facilitator directs the observers to present their observations on group interactions to the total group. There is no discussion at this point.

XIII. With the aid of HELPCO's process consultation, the management firm attempts to create an improved design that is acceptable to the client. HELPCO members attempt to implement their consultation strategy and aid the management firm members in functioning more effectively. During this time, the bank representatives react further to the proposal they have seen and the comments made, reconsider their criteria, and prepare to make a final decision.

XIV. If the management firm has succeeded in formulating a final program proposal, it is presented to the bank representatives who discuss among themselves whether to accept or reject the proposal, depending on their evaluation of it. The bank representatives then inform the management firm of their decision and give a brief summary of their reasons for the decisions. (Ten minutes.)

XV. The process observers again report what they have observed to the entire group.

XVI. The facilitator leads a discussion of the feedback from the observers, individual experiences during the role play, and the experience as a whole. Participants may separate into four groups (management systems firm management, management design teams, bank representatives, and HELPCO team) to continue the discussion and then report their conclusions to the total group. (These discussions should be focused on the process of OD consultation and the development of OD diagnosis, consultation, and observation skills.)

Variations

I. The situation can be rewritten to suit the professional backgrounds of the participants.

II. Each process observer can be instructed to report only to the group that he observed.

Similar Structured Experiences: *Vol. IV:* Structured Experience **111;** *'74 Annual:* **131;** *'75 Annual:* **144;** *'76 Annual:* **183.**

Lecturette Sources: *'72 Annual:* "McGregor's Theory X-Theory Y Model"; *'74 Annual:* "The 'Shouldist' Manager"; *'75 Annual:* "Participatory Management: A New Morality"; *'76 Annual:* "A Current Assessment of OD: What It Is and Why It Often Fails"; *'77 Annual:* "Organizational Norms," "Consulting Process in Action."

Notes on the Use of "HELPCO":

Submitted by Neil E. Rand.

PARTICIPANT ROLE-DESCRIPTION SHEET

Each role with its corresponding description should be printed on a separate 3″ x 5″ card and distributed at random to the participants from each group. Each participant should see only his card and no other. The word or phrase that follows each role is a description of the predominant aspect of that person's character, but it should be explained that the person playing that role is not limited to that description alone and may expand it at his own discretion.

Role	*Description*
Management Systems Firm President	Dynamic, overbearing, controlling, hard-hitting entrepreneur.
Management Systems Firm Vice President	"Deadwood," no real role in company, only there because he is the president's brother-in-law, interfering.
Management Systems Firm Manager	Bureaucratic, wants things done exactly right so that he can please the president.
Management Design Team 1 Leader:	Autocratic, very controlling.
Management Design Team 2 Leader:	Democratic, sympathetic to others.
Management Design Team 3 Leader:	Laissez-faire, exerts little or no leadership.
Management Design Team 1: Designer A	Ambitious.
Management Design Team 1: Designer B	Hostile.
Management Design Team 1: Designer C	Sympathetic and eager to please.
Management Design Team 2: Designer A	Confrontive and argumentative.

Management Design Team 2: Designer B	Placating and overly agreeable.
Management Design Team 2: Designer C	Overly intellectual.
Management Design Team 3: Designer A	Lazy.
Management Design Team 3: Designer B	Competitive.
Management Design Team 3: Designer C	Overly talkative about anything.
Management Design Team 4: Designer A	Easily distracted.
Management Design Team 4: Designer B	Anxious, easily worried.
Management Design Team 4: Designer C	Task oriented, hard working.
Chairman of the Board, First Town Bank	Bureaucratic, worried about cost.
Vice President for Development, First Town Bank	Progressive, wants bank to be more dynamic.
Board Member, First Town Bank	Conservative, traditional, sceptical of "touchy-feely" approaches to development.

MANAGEMENT SYSTEMS FIRM BACKGROUND SHEET

(To be distributed to members of the management firm and their observer.)

History

Your organization was founded by its president, an engineer, who saw a need for management systems design that was suited to the organizational requirements of businesses, and he created this firm to meet this need. The firm prospered and expanded to its present size in a short time. However, economic conditions have changed, clients are not paying their bills, leaving the company in a bad financial position. Things have become so bad that the president's brother-in-law—who knows little about this business but who supplied a large share of the initial capital—has become vice president in order to help straighten things out.

Present Situation

The firm has just interested a prospective client, the First Town Bank, in designing a training program in problem solving for its management personnel. All of the firm's employees know that their company is desperate and that they must satisfy this potential client in order to stay in business.

Corporate Mission

It must be determined what the representatives of the bank want and what is required in order to present them with a design proposal for a training program that will be acceptable to them. The design teams will independently create proposals, of which only one will be presented to the client. The president of your company has already offered a large bonus to the design team with the best proposal (conditional to its being accepted by the client), and has let it be known that design teams with less suitable proposals may be faced with layoffs.

ORGANIZATIONAL CHART

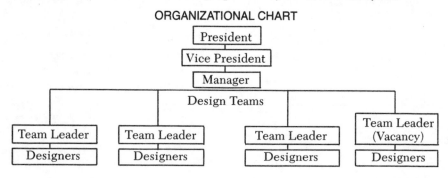

MANAGEMENT SYSTEMS FIRM INSTRUCTION SHEET

(To be distributed to members of the management firm and their observer.)

Your firm will be named after the president of the company, e.g., Smith and Associates, Inc.

Your initial task is to decide:
1. How the job will be handled;
2. Who will meet with the client (bank) representatives;
3. Who will instruct the design teams about what they must do.

Any member of your organization may call in the consultation team from HELPCO at any time, but the president of your firm must call in HELPCO if no one has yet done so before a proposal is submitted to the client representatives.

You will first submit a preliminary proposal to the bank representatives. Following their critique, you will submit a final proposal, which they may accept or reject.

CLIENT INSTRUCTION SHEET

(To be distributed to representatives of the First Town Bank and their observer.)

You are a representative of the First Town Bank. There are three members of your group: the chairman of the board, the vice president for development, and a member of the board of directors.

When directed to do so, your group will contact the members of a management systems firm, apprise them of your bank's needs for a training program in problem solving for your managers, and ask them for a proposal.

You will have an opportunity to review two proposals submitted by the management firm. The first will be a preliminary proposal, which you may critique, making any suggestions or criticisms that you feel are appropriate. The second proposal will be a final proposal, which you may accept or reject on behalf of your bank.

Before you initiate this transaction, you are to reach some consensus with regard to your bank's training needs and objectives at this time.

Structured Experience 211

HELPCO CONSULTANT INSTRUCTION SHEET

(To be distributed to members of HELPCO and their observer.)

You are members of an organization development consulting firm, HELPCO. You will be contacted by a management systems firm to aid it in the design of a training program in problem solving for management for its client, the First Town Bank.

You have no prescribed roles, but you are to act according to what you believe is suitable for your own firm and your client.

The facilitator will function as a senior but equal member of your consultant staff. He will not accompany you when you meet with the members of the management firm but he will be available to discuss consultation problems with you.

Your initial task is to discuss your philosophy of consultation. You may continue this discussion until you are called in by the members of the management firm.

212. MURDER ONE: INFORMATION SHARING

Goals

I. To explore the effects of cooperation-collaboration versus competition in group problem solving.

II. To demonstrate the need for information sharing and other problem-solving strategies in a task-oriented group.

III. To study the roles that emerge in a task group.

Group Size

At least two groups of five members each.

Time Required

One and one-half hours.

Materials

I. A copy of the Murder One Instruction Sheet for each participant.

II. A copy of the Murder One Suspect Data Sheet for each participant.

III. One set of Murder One Briefing Sheets for each group, a different sheet for each member. (Each of the five sheets is coded by the number of dots, ranging from one to five, at the end of the first and last paragraphs. Each sheet contains data that is not found on another sheet in that set.)

IV. Blank paper and a pencil for each participant.

V. A Murder One Solution Sheet for each participant.

VI. Newsprint and a felt-tipped marker.

Physical Setting

A room large enough for groups to meet simultaneously without disturbing each other or overhearing each other's solutions to the problem. Each group should have a table and chairs at which the members may work. (An alternative is to have a separate room for each group, in which it can work during the problem-solving phase.)

Process

I. The facilitator introduces the activity as a group problem-solving task. (He does *not* discuss at this time the need to share information.)

II. The facilitator divides the participants into groups of five members each. If there are four or less participants remaining, they may serve as process consultants.

III. The facilitator explains that each group's task is to decide who is the suspect to be arrested on a charge of first-degree murder. He indicates that there is only one correct solution to the problem and that each group is to reach its decision independent of the other groups. He also says that when a group completes the task, its members may observe other groups still in process, but they may not interfere with or join the other group in any way.

IV. The facilitator distributes a Murder One Instruction Sheet, Briefing Sheet, and Suspect Data Sheet, as well as paper and a pencil to each participant. He takes care to see that each member of a group has received a different Briefing Sheet (with a different number of dots following the first and last paragraphs).

V. The facilitator may privately brief any process consultants on what to look for during the group process. They are instructed to intervene as they deem necessary to help a group to clarify its *process*, and they are told not to participate in the group's discussion of the *content*. The facilitator then tells the groups that they have forty-five minutes in which to solve the problem and that they are to record their reasons for *eliminating* each suspect. He gives the signal to begin.

VI. When all groups have reached a decision, or at the end of forty-five minutes, the entire group is reassembled. Each group reports on its solution, and the facilitator may briefly outline the elimination process on newsprint. Then the Murder One Solution Sheets are distributed and explained.

VII. The facilitator then leads a discussion of the experience, focusing on the effects of collaboration and competition, the need to share information in problem solving, the roles that were played by group members, and other task-related strategies or group dynamics.

Variations

I. The situation and information can be adapted to suit the needs and background of the group.

II. Observers can be assigned to specific groups or can be directed to look for specific aspects of the group process.

III. The facilitator can inform the participants that the data sheets contain different information.

IV. The facilitator can increase competition between groups by posting the amount of time used by each group in accomplishing its task and by posting the solution arrived at by each group.

Similar Structured Experiences: *Vol. I:* Structured Experience **12;** *Vol. II:* **31;** *'72 Annual:* **80;** *'73 Annual:* **98;** *Vol. IV:* **103, 117;** *'74 Annual:* **133, 135;** *'75 Annual:* **139;** *Vol. V:* **155, 156;** *'76 Annual:* **178;** *'77 Annual:* **192.**

Lecturette Sources: *'73 Annual:* "Conditions Which Hinder Effective Communication"; *'74 Annual:* "Five Components Contributing to Effective Interpersonal Communications," "Hidden Agendas"; *'76 Annual:* "Clarity of Expression in Interpersonal Communication."

Notes on the Use of "Murder One":

Submitted by Donald K. McLeod.

Structured Experience 212

MURDER ONE INSTRUCTION SHEET

Instructions:

1. The threat of violence between various factions of organized crime, over the control of narcotics, imperils the tranquility of your community. To combat this threat, the commissioner has directed a step-up in the activity against criminal organizations within your community.
2. You are a group of top detectives who have been assigned to the Organized Crime Bureau within your department.
3. Charly "Poppa" Hasson's gang has been singled out for particular attention by your team.
4. Your task becomes complicated when murder occurs during your investigation.
5. Your task, as a group, is to single out one suspect from members of the Hasson gang. Circumstantial evidence may be used to identify and arrest one member of the gang. The remaining six suspects must be cleared for a specific reason, which you as a group must declare at the termination of the activity. Data has been supplied regarding the suspects. Your team has all the information necessary for the solution of the case.

Assumptions:

1. Assume that there is one solution.
2. Assume that all data are correct.
3. You have forty-five minutes in which to determine a suspect.
4. Assume that today's date is July 7, 1977 and that all primary actions are taking place on this date.
5. There must be substantial agreement in your group that the problem is solved.
6. You must work the problem as a group.

MURDER ONE SUSPECT DATA SHEET

Viron, Benjamin ("Benjie")   M-W-49
Height: 5'4"   Weight: 220   Hair: Gray/Brown   Eyes: Brown
Blood Type: B   Shoe: 7½ D   Tattoos: Right arm, "Mother"
Vehicle: 1973 Mercedes Dark Blue Sedan
Record: 17 arrests—Charges: Gambling, Loansharking, Extortion, Assault,
                          Narcotics, Robbery, Rape.

Enopac, Alphonse ("Jumbo")   M-W-52
Height: 5'7"   Weight: 245   Hair: Black/Gray   Eyes: Brown
Blood Type: A   Shoe: 8 D   Tattoos: Left arm, "Al & Eloise"
Vehicle: 1974 Lincoln Black Sedan
Record: 26 arrests—Charges: Gambling, Narcotics, Extortion, Assault, Statutory
                          Rape, Homicide.

Ollag, Joseph ("Chills")   M-W-52
Height: 5'7½"   Weight: 180   Hair: Brown   Eyes: Brown
Blood Type: A   Shoe: 8 D   Tattoos: None
Vehicle: 1972 Cadillac Black Sedan
Record: 20 arrests—Charges: Gambling, Narcotics, Assault, Extortion,
                          Homicide.

Phelps, James ("Digger")   M-W-52
Height: 5'7"   Weight: 210   Hair: Black/Brown   Eyes: Blue
Blood Type: B   Shoe: 7½ D   Tattoos: Chest, "Blue Birds"
Vehicle: 1973 Cadillac Dark Green Sedan
Record: 30 arrests—Charges: Gambling, Narcotics, Assault, Robbery,
                          Loansharking, Homicide.

Sutter, Edward ("Blue Eyes")   M-W-51
Height: 5'7"   Weight: 240   Hair: Black/Gray   Eyes: Brown
Blood Type: B   Shoe: 7½ D   Tattoos: Right Arm,
                          "For God & Country"
Vehicle: 1974 Chrysler Black Sedan
Record: 12 arrests—Charges: Gambling, Loansharking, Assault, Rape, Extortion.

Structured Experience 212

Lagas, Franklin ("Hot Dog")   M-W-50
Height: 5'7"   Weight: 235   Hair: Black/Gray   Eyes: Brown
Blood Type: B   Shoe: 8 D   Tattoos: None
Vehicle: 1973 Cadillac Black Sedan
Record: 19 arrests—Charges: Homicide, Robbery, Assault, Extortion, Narcotics,
          Gambling, Impairing Morals of a Minor.

Aifam, George ("Gypsy")   M-W-39
Height: 5'7½"   Weight: 245   Hair: Black   Eyes: Brown
Blood Type: B   Shoe: 8 D   Tattoos: Left arm,
          "To Mother With Love"
Vehicle: 1973 Lincoln Black Sedan
Record: 23 arrests—Charges: Gambling, Loansharking, Assault, Extortion,
          Homicide.

MURDER ONE BRIEFING SHEET

Charly "Poppa" Hasson has been linked to organized crime by both Federal and state Organized Crime Task Forces. Information has been received that Poppa Hasson has formed a gang of his own and is engaged in heavyweight narcotics traffic. Recent investigations by your department have disclosed the identity of seven members of the Hasson gang. Further investigations and surveillance have revealed that the members of the gang are actively engaged in narcotics distribution despite severe pressure from the Joint Organized Task Force. Confidential information has disclosed a widening rift between gang members and Charly Hasson; members of the gang have accused him of "skimming off the top." Threats have been made by gang members to blow Charly away if he doesn't shape up.

As a result of the threats, Poppa has been making himself scarce and rarely meets more than one gang member at a time. He has secluded himself in an apartment in a remote part of town, a relatively safe location unknown to the gang members. An informant has told your department about Hasson's hideout, and a legal wiretap has been installed on his telephone. Several days have gone by, and no action has been indicated by the tap. On July 7, at 7:03 p.m., Charly made a call to an undetermined public phone booth, and a taped conversation was recorded as follows:

Unknown Person: "Yeah?"

Poppa (Charly): "Eh, I got a big one; meet me at the club at 10:30."

Unknown Person: "O.K." (Clicks off.)

Past information indicates the club to be the Starlight Hunting & Fishing Club at 197 Kenmore Street, a secluded place used in the past for gang meetings. Other persons have divulged that some heavyweight drugs have come into town. Thus, it appears that Poppa may be getting a slice of the action. With this in mind, your squad C.O. decides to cover the club and put a close surveillance on all suspects at the location.

The Joint Task Force, having information confirming a big shipment to the city, swings into action at 9:00 p.m. this date and simultaneously rounds up suspects who might be involved. The sweep nets twenty suspects, including Johnny Blue Eyes, Harry Hinge, Bruce Comma, Benny Carato, Sam Perez, John Smith, Mike Crupa, Danny Skidmore, Frankie Todd, Sidney Hall, Jackie Leod, and Cary Crooke. All are known by the department to be actively engaged in illegal narcotics traffic. The stakeout at Poppa's house reports that he leaves at 9:30 p.m., but he loses the tail at about 10:00 p.m. on the other side of town. Other tails report in, and information about the members of Poppa's gang is compiled by the team. At 7:00 p.m., surveillance had disclosed that Jumbo and Benjie's whereabouts were unknown; Hot Dog and Gypsy were near an offtrack

Structured Experience 212

betting office, Digger was at some meeting, and Chills and Blue Eyes were in the vicinity of a social club. Armed with this information, the team moves to 197 Kenmore Street.

At 10:15 p.m., the first unit of the team arrives and observes that the club door is ajar and Hasson's car is parked outside. The area seems deserted, and only one light flickers through the open door. It appears from the outside that someone is lying on the floor. A decision is made to move in for a better look. Closer scrutiny reveals Charly's body lying face down on the floor. He is bleeding profusely from head wounds—apparently gunshot wounds from a weapon found lying near an open window at the rear of the premises. The area is immediately sealed off, and the forensic unit is called to the scene. While awaiting the results of the lab unit, the team makes a door-to-door canvas in an attempt to locate a witness or persons who might have seen Charly "Poppa" with someone at the location. The search is apparently fruitless until one middle-aged man is found who observed two men entering the abandoned club while he was walking his dog. The frightened witness, who resides three blocks from the club, says he saw the two enter the building and then heard a loud argument, during which someone shouted "No! No!" At that time he heard two shots, and the door of the club opened but no one came out. Then he saw a man fleeing from behind the building. The man was middle-aged, wore a white shirt and black trousers, was about average in height, and was heavy. The man fled in a dark sedan parked on the next block. The witness, fearful for his own life, ran home, and when a detective doing door-to-door interviews came to his house, the witness gave him the above information.

The forensic unit thoroughly searches the premises and comes up with prints belonging to Poppa; other prints are not distinguishable and cannot be classified. The weapon located at the scene is a .44 magnum of undetermined origin—no prints are obtained from the gun. Blood stains seem to indicate a fierce struggle, and apparently Charly had almost made it to the door. The blood stains on the floor fall into two groupings: A and B. Charly had bled profusely; he had blood type A. Beneath his fingernails are tufts of hair. Further investigation reveals a footprint in the tomato patch below the window at the rear of the club. The print seems to be anywhere from a size 7 D to a size 8 D; it is somewhat distorted and was made by a man of greater-than-average weight. (This is determined by a mold made at the scene and a measurement of the height of the drop from the window to the ground.) Pressure from the hierarchy of the department demands a quick solution to this case, especially in view of the recent mass arrests made by the Joint Task Force. On the basis of the facts herein your team is directed to make a prompt arrest.

The most likely suspects are the members of Charly "Poppa" Hasson's gang. It would seem likely that Charly called a member of the gang and made an appointment with his killer. All the information available to your team can be culled from the Briefing Sheet. Your task is to identify the killer by using the facts available.

MURDER ONE BRIEFING SHEET

Charly "Poppa" Hasson has been linked to organized crime by both Federal and state Organized Crime Task Forces. Information has been received that Poppa Hasson has formed a gang of his own and is engaged in heavyweight narcotics traffic. Recent investigations by your department have disclosed the identity of seven members of the Hasson gang. Further investigations and surveillance have revealed that the members of the gang are actively engaged in narcotics distribution despite severe pressure from the Joint Organized Task Force. Confidential information has disclosed a widening rift between gang members and Charly Hasson; members of the gang have accused him of "skimming off the top." Threats have been made by gang members to blow Charly away if he doesn't shape up . .

As a result of the threats, Poppa has been making himself scarce and rarely meets more than one gang member at a time. He has secluded himself in an apartment in a remote part of town, a relatively safe location unknown to the gang members. An informant has told your department about Hasson's hideout, and a legal wiretap has been installed on his telephone. Several days have gone by, and no action has been indicated by the tap. On July 7, at 7:03 p.m., Charly made a call to an undetermined public phone booth, and a taped conversation was recorded as follows:

Unknown Person: "Yeah?"

Poppa (Charly): "Eh, I got a big one; meet me at the club at 10:30."

Unknown Person: "O.K." (Clicks off.)

Past information indicates the club to be the Starlight Hunting & Fishing Club at 197 Kenmore Street, a secluded place used in the past for gang meetings. Other information has divulged that some heavyweight drugs have come into town. Thus, it appears that Poppa may be getting a slice of the action. With this in mind, your squad C.O. decides to cover the club and put a close surveillance on all suspects at the location.

The Joint Task Force, having information confirming a big shipment to the city, swings into action at 9:00 p.m. this date and simultaneously rounds up suspects who might be involved. The sweep nets twenty suspects, including Johnny Blue Eyes, Harry Hinge, Bruce Comma, Benny Carato, Sam Perez, John Smith, Mike Crupa, Danny Skidmore, Frankie Todd, Sidney Hall, Jackie Leod, and Cary Crooke. All are known by the department to be actively engaged in illegal narcotics traffic. The stakeout at Poppa's house reports that he leaves at 9:30 p.m., but he loses the tail at about 10:00 p.m. on the other side of town. Other tails report in, and information about the members of Poppa's gang is compiled by the team. At 7:00 p.m., surveillance had disclosed that Jumbo and Benjie's whereabouts were unknown; Hot Dog and Gypsy were near an offtrack

betting office, Digger was at some meeting, and Chills and Blue Eyes were in the vicinity of a social club. Armed with this information, the team moves to 197 Kenmore Street.

At 10:15 p.m., the first unit of the team arrives and observes that the club door is ajar and Hasson's car is parked outside. The area seems deserted, and only one light flickers through the open door. It appears from the outside that someone is lying on the floor. A decision is made to move in for a better look. Closer scrutiny reveals Charly's body lying face down on the floor. He is bleeding profusely from head wounds—apparently gunshot wounds from a weapon found lying near an open window at the rear of the premises. The area is immediately sealed off, and the forensic unit is called to the scene. While awaiting the results of the lab unit, the team makes a door-to-door canvas in an attempt to locate a witness or persons who might have seen Charly "Poppa" with someone at the location. The search is apparently fruitless until one middle-aged man is found who observed two men entering the abandoned club while he was walking his dog. The frightened witness, who resides three blocks from the club, says he saw the two enter the building and then heard a loud argument, during which someone shouted "No! No!" At that time he heard two shots, and the door of the club opened but no one came out. Then he saw a man fleeing from behind the building. The man was about fifty, wore a white shirt and black trousers, was about average in height, and was heavy. The man fled in a dark sedan parked on the next block. The witness, fearful for his own life, ran home, and when a detective doing door-to-door interviews came to his house, the witness gave him the above information.

The forensic unit thoroughly searches the premises and comes up with prints belonging to Poppa; other prints are not distinguishable and cannot be classified. The weapon located at the scene is a .44 magnum of undetermined origin—no prints are obtained from the gun. Blood stains seem to indicate a fierce struggle, and apparently Charly had almost made it to the door. The blood stains on the floor fall into two groupings: A and B. Charly had bled profusely and beneath his fingernails are tufts of hair. Further investigation reveals a footprint in the tomato patch below the window at the rear of the club. The print seems to be anywhere from a size 7 D to a size 8 D; it is somewhat distorted and was made by a man of over two hundred pounds in weight. (This is determined by a mold made at the scene and a measurement of the height of the drop from the window to the ground.) Pressure from the hierarchy of the department demands a quick solution to the case, especially in view of the recent mass arrests made by the Joint Task Force. On the basis of the facts herein your team is directed to make a prompt arrest.

The most likely suspects are the members of Charly "Poppa" Hasson's gang. It would seem likely that Charly called a member of the gang and made an appointment with his killer. All the information available to your team can be culled from the Briefing Sheet. Your task is to identify the killer by using the facts available . .

MURDER ONE BRIEFING SHEET

Charly "Poppa" Hasson has been linked to organized crime by both Federal and state Organized Crime Task Forces. Information has been received that Poppa Hasson has formed a gang of his own and is engaged in heavyweight narcotics traffic. Recent investigations by your department have disclosed the identity of seven members of the Hasson gang. Further investigations and surveillance have revealed that the members of the gang are actively engaged in narcotics distribution despite severe pressure from the Joint Organized Task Force. Confidential information has disclosed a widening rift between gang members and Charly Hasson; members of the gang have accused him of "skimming off the top." Threats have been made by gang members to blow Charly away if he doesn't shape up . . .

As a result of the threats, Poppa has been making himself scarce and rarely meets more than one gang member at a time. He has secluded himself in an apartment in a remote part of town, a relatively safe location unknown to the gang members. An informant has told your department about Hasson's hideout, and a legal wiretap has been installed on his telephone. Several days have gone by, and no action has been indicated by the tap. On July 7, at 7:03 p.m., Charly made a call to an undetermined public phone booth, and a taped conversation was recorded as follows:

Unknown Person: "Yeah?"

Poppa (Charly): "Eh, I got a big one; meet me at the club at 10:30."

Unknown Person: "O.K." (Clicks off.)

Past information indicates the club to be the Starlight Hunting & Fishing Club at 197 Kenmore Street, a secluded place used in the past for gang meetings. Other persons have divulged that some heavyweight drugs have come into town. Thus, it appears that Poppa may be getting a slice of the action. With this in mind, your squad C.O. decides to cover the club and put a close surveillance on all suspects at the location.

The Joint Task Force, having information confirming a big shipment to the city, swings into action at 9:00 p.m. this date and simultaneously rounds up suspects who might be involved. The sweep nets twenty suspects, including Johnny Blue Eyes, Harry Hinge, Bruce Comma, Benny Carato, Sam Perez, John Smith, Mike Crupa, Danny Skidmore, Frankie Todd, Sidney Hall, Jackie Leod, and Cary Crooke. All are known by the department to be actively engaged in illegal narcotics traffic. The stakeout at Poppa's house reports that he leaves at 9:30 p.m., but he loses the tail at about 10:00 p.m. on the other side of town. Other tails report in, and information about the members of Poppa's gang is compiled by the team. At 7:00 p.m., surveillance had disclosed that Jumbo and Benjie's whereabouts were unknown; Hot Dog and Gypsy were near an offtrack

betting office, Digger was at some meeting, and Chills and Blue Eyes were in the vicinity of a social club. Armed with this information, the team moves to 197 Kenmore Street.

At 10:15 p.m., the first unit of the team arrives and observes that the club door is ajar and Hasson's car is parked outside. The area seems deserted, and only one light flickers through the open door. It appears from the outside that someone is lying on the floor. A decision is made to move in for a better look. Closer scrutiny reveals Charly's body lying face down on the floor. He is bleeding profusely from head wounds—apparently gunshot wounds from a weapon found lying near an open window at the rear of the premises. The area is immediately sealed off, and the forensic unit is called to the scene. While awaiting the results of the lab unit, the team makes a door-to-door canvas in an attempt to locate a witness or persons who might have seen Charly "Poppa" with someone at the location. The search is apparently fruitless until one middle-aged man is found who observed two men entering the abandoned club while he was walking his dog. The frightened witness, who resides three blocks from the club, says he saw the two enter the building and then heard a loud argument, during which someone shouted "No! No!" At that time he heard two shots, and the door of the club opened but no one came out. Then he saw a man fleeing from behind the building. The man was middle-aged, wore a white shirt and black trousers, was about five feet seven, and was heavy. The man fled in a dark sedan parked on the next block. The witness, fearful for his own life, ran home, and when a detective doing door-to-door interviews came to his house, the witness gave him the above information.

The forensic unit thoroughly searches the premises and comes up with prints belonging to Poppa; other prints are not distinguishable and cannot be classified. The weapon located at the scene was a .44 magnum of undetermined origin—no prints were obtained from the gun. Blood stains seem to indicate a fierce struggle, and apparently Charly had almost made it to the door. The blood stains on the floor fall into two groupings: A and B. Charly had bled profusely and beneath his fingernails is a tuft of hair. Further investigation reveals a footprint in the tomato patch below the window at the rear of the club. The print seems to be anywhere from a size 7 D to a size 8 D; it is somewhat distorted and was made by a man of greater-than-average weight. (This is determined by a mold made at the scene and a measurement of the height of the drop from the window to the ground.) Pressure from the hierarchy of the department demands a quick solution to this case, especially in view of the recent mass arrests made by the Joint Task Force. On the basis of the facts herein your team is directed to make a prompt arrest.

The most likely suspects are the members of Charly "Poppa" Hasson's gang. It would seem likely that Charly called a member of the gang and made an appointment with his killer. All the information available to your team can be culled from the Briefing Sheet. Your task is to identify the killer by using the facts available . . .

MURDER ONE BRIEFING SHEET

Charly "Poppa" Hasson has been linked to organized crime by both Federal and state Organized Crime Task Forces. Information has been received that Poppa Hasson has formed a gang of his own and is engaged in heavyweight narcotics traffic. Recent investigations by your department have disclosed the identity of seven members of the Hasson gang. Further investigations and surveillance have revealed that the members of the gang are actively engaged in narcotics distribution despite severe pressure from the Joint Organized Task Force. Confidential information has disclosed a widening rift between gang members and Charly Hasson; members of the gang have accused him of "skimming off the top." Threats have been made by gang members to blow Charly away if he doesn't shape up . . . .

As a result of the threats, Poppa has been making himself scarce and rarely meets more than one gang member at a time. He has secluded himself in an apartment in a remote part of town, a relatively safe location unknown to the gang members. An informant has told your department about Hasson's hideout, and a legal wiretap has been installed on his telephone. Several days have gone by, and no action has been indicated by the tap. On July 7, at 7:03 p.m., Charly made a call to an undetermined public phone booth, and a taped conversation was recorded as follows:

Unknown Person: "Yeah?"
Poppa (Charly): "Eh, I got a big one; meet me at the club at 10:30."
Unknown Person: "O.K." (Clicks off.)

Past information indicates the club to be the Starlight Hunting & Fishing Club at 197 Kenmore Street, a secluded place used in the past for gang meetings. Other persons have divulged that some heavyweight drugs have come into town. Thus, it appears that Poppa may be getting a slice of the action. With this in mind, your squad C.O. decides to cover the club and put a close surveillance on all suspects at the location.

The Joint Task Force, having information confirming a big shipment to the city, swings into action at 9:00 p.m. this date and simultaneously rounds up suspects who might be involved. The sweep nets twenty suspects, including Johnny Blue Eyes, Harry Hinge, Bruce Comma, Benny Carato, Frankie Lagas, Sam Perez, John Smith, Mike Crupa, Danny Skidmore, Frankie Todd, Sidney Hall, Jackie Leod, and Cary Crooke. All are known by the department to be actively engaged in illegal narcotics traffic. The stakeout at Poppa's house reports that he leaves at 9:30 p.m., but he loses the tail at about 10:00 p.m. on the other side of town. Other tails report in, and information about the members of Poppa's gang is compiled by the team. At 7:00 p.m., surveillance had disclosed that Jumbo and Benjie's whereabouts were unknown; Hot Dog and Gypsy were near

Structured Experience 212

an offtrack betting office, Digger was at some meeting, and Chills and Blue Eyes were in the vicinity of a social club. Armed with this information, the team moves to 197 Kenmore Street.

At 10:15 p.m., the first unit of the team arrives and observes that the club door is ajar and Hasson's car is parked outside. The area seems deserted, and only one light flickers through the open door. It appears from the outside that someone is lying on the floor. A decision is made to move in for a better look. Closer scrutiny reveals Charly's body lying face down on the floor. He is bleeding profusely from head wounds—apparently gunshot wounds from a weapon found lying near an open window at the rear of the premises. The area is immediately sealed off, and the forensic unit is called to the scene. While awaiting the results of the lab unit, the team makes a door-to-door canvas in an attempt to locate a witness or persons who might have seen Charly "Poppa" with someone at the location. The search is apparently fruitless until one middle-aged man is found who observed two men entering the abandoned club while he was walking his dog. The frightened witness, who resides three blocks from the club, says he saw the two enter the building and then heard a loud argument, during which someone shouted "No! No!" At that time he heard two shots, and the door of the club opened but no one came out. Then he saw a man fleeing from behind the building. The man was middle-aged, wore a white shirt and black trousers, was about average in height, and was heavy. The man fled in a dark sedan parked on the next block. The witness, fearful for his own life, ran home, and when a detective doing door-to-door interviews came to his house, the witness gave him the above information.

The forensic unit throughly searches the premises and comes up with prints belonging to Poppa; other prints are not distinguishable and cannot be classified. The weapon located at the scene is a .44 magnum of undetermined origin—no prints are obtained from the gun. Blood stains seem to indicate a fierce struggle, and apparently Charly had almost made it to the door. The blood stains on the floor fall into two groupings: A and B. Charly had bled profusely and beneath his fingernails are tufts of hair. Further investigation reveals a footprint in the tomato patch below the window at the rear of the club. The print seems to be anywhere from a size 7 D to a size 8 D; it is somewhat distorted and was made by a man of greater-than-average weight. (This is determined by a mold made at the scene and a measurement of the height of the drop from the window to the ground.) Pressure from the hierarchy of the department demands a quick solution to this case, especially in view of the recent mass arrests made by the Joint Task Force. On the basis of the facts herein your team is directed to make a prompt arrest.

The most likely suspects are the members of Charly "Poppa" Hasson's gang. It would seem likely that Charly called a member of the gang and made an appointment with his killer. All the information available to your team can be culled from the Briefing Sheet. Your task is to identify the killer by using the facts available . . . .

MURDER ONE BRIEFING SHEET

Charly "Poppa" Hasson has been linked to organized crime by both Federal and state Organized Crime Task Forces. Information has been received that Poppa Hasson has formed a gang of his own and is engaged in heavyweight narcotics traffic. Recent investigations by your department have disclosed the identity of seven members of the Hasson gang. Further investigations and surveillance have revealed that the members of the gang are actively engaged in narcotics distribution despite severe pressure from the Joint Organized Task Force. Confidential information has disclosed a widening rift between gang members and Charly Hasson; members of the gang have accused him of "skimming off the top." Threats have been made by gang members to blow Charly away if he doesn't shape up . . . . .

As a result of the threats, Poppa has been making himself scarce and rarely meets more than one gang member at a time. He has secluded himself in an apartment in a remote part of town, a relatively safe location unknown to the gang members. An informant has told your department about Hasson's hideout, and a legal wiretap has been installed on his telephone. Several days have gone by, and no action has been indicated by the tap. On July 7, at 7:03 p.m., Charly made a call to an undetermined public phone booth, and a taped conversation was recorded as follows:

Unknown Person: "Yeah?"

Poppa (Charly): "Eh, I got a big one; meet me at the club at 10:30."

Unknown Person: "O.K." (Clicks off.)

Past information indicates the club to be the Starlight Hunting & Fishing Club at 197 Kenmore Street, a secluded place used in the past for gang meetings. Other persons have divulged that some heavyweight drugs have come into town. Thus, it appears that Poppa may be getting a slice of the action. With this in mind, your squad C.O. decides to cover the club and put a close surveillance on all suspects at the location.

The Joint Task Force, having information confirming a big shipment to the city, swings into action at 9:00 p.m. this date and simultaneously rounds up suspects who might be involved. The sweep nets twenty suspects, including Johnny Blue Eyes, Harry Hinge, Bruce Comma, Benny Carato, Sam Perez, John Smith, Mike Crupa, Danny Skidmore, Frankie Todd, Sidney Hall, Jackie Leod, and Cary Crooke. All are known by the department to be actively engaged in illegal narcotics traffic. The stakeout at Poppa's house reports that he leaves at 9:30 p.m., but he loses the tail at about 10:00 p.m. on the other side of town. Other tails report in, and information about the members of Poppa's gang is compiled by the team. At 7:00 p.m., surveillance had disclosed that Jumbo and Benjie's whereabouts were unknown; Hot Dog and Gypsy were near an offtrack

Structured Experience 212

betting office, Digger was conducting a union meeting, and Chills and Blue Eyes were in the vicinity of a social club. Armed with this information, the team moves to 197 Kenmore Street.

At 10:15 p.m., the first unit of the team arrives and observes that the club door is ajar and Hasson's car is parked outside. The area seems deserted, and only one light flickers through the open door. It appears from the outside that someone is lying on the floor. A decision is made to move in for a better look. Closer scrutiny reveals Charly's body lying face down on the floor. He is bleeding profusely from head wounds—apparently gunshot wounds from a weapon found lying near an open window at the rear of the premises. The area is immediately sealed off, and the forensic unit is called to the scene. While awaiting the results of the lab unit, the team makes a door-to-door canvas in an attempt to locate a witness or persons who might have seen Charly "Poppa" with someone at the location. The search is apparently fruitless until one middle-aged man is found who observed two men entering the abandoned club while he was walking his dog. The frightened witness, who resides three blocks from the club, says he saw the two enter the building and then heard a loud argument, during which someone shouted "No! No!" At that time he heard two shots, and the door of the club opened but no one came out. Then he saw a man fleeing from behind the building. The man was middle-aged, wore a white shirt and black trousers, was about average in height, and was heavy. The man fled in a dark sedan parked on the next block. The witness, fearful for his own life, ran home, and when a detective doing door-to-door interviews came to his house, the witness gave him the above information.

The forensic unit thoroughly searches the premises and comes up with prints belonging to Poppa; other prints are not distinguishable and cannot be classified. The weapon located at the scene is a .44 magnum of undetermined origin—no prints are obtained from the gun. Blood stains seem to indicate a fierce struggle, and apparently Charly had almost made it to the door. The blood stains on the floor fall into two groupings: A and B. Charly had bled profusely and beneath his fingernails are tufts of hair. Further investigation revealed a footprint in the tomato patch below the window at the rear of the club. The print seems to be anywhere from a size 7 D to a size 8 D; it is somewhat distorted and was made by a man of greater-than-average weight. (This is determined by a mold made at the scene and a measurement of the height of the drop from the window to the ground.) Pressure from the hierarchy of the department demands a quick solution to this case, especially in view of the recent mass arrests made by the Joint Task Force. On the basis of the facts herein your team is directed to make a prompt arrest.

The most likely suspects are the members of Charly "Poppa" Hasson's gang. It would seem likely that Charly called a member of the gang and made an appointment with his killer. All the information available to your team can be culled from the Briefing Sheet. Your task is to identify the killer by using the facts available . . . . .

MURDER ONE SOLUTION SHEET

(Note: Items printed in bold face indicate why the suspect could not have committed the crime. Everyone is eliminated except . . .

Name	Height	Weight	Age	Blood Type	Occupation at 7 p.m. (free to make phone call)	Occupation at 10 p.m. (free to commit murder)
Viron, Benjamin ("Benjie")	**5'4"**	220	49	B	unknown	unknown
Enopac, Alphonse ("Jumbo")	5'7"	245	52	**A**	unknown	unknown
Ollag, Joseph ("Chills")	5'7½"	**180**	52	**A**	near social club	unknown
Phelps, James ("Digger")	5'7"	210	52	B	**conducting union meeting**	unknown
Sutter, Edward ("Blue Eyes")	5'7"	240	51	B	near social club	unknown
Lagas, Franklin ("Hot Dog")	5'7"	235	50	B	near offtrack betting office	**in custody of Joint Task Force**
Aifam, George ("Gypsy")	5'7½"	245	39	B	near offtrack betting office	unknown

Structured Experience 212

213. SHERLOCK: AN INFERENCE ACTIVITY

Goals

   I. To increase awareness of how prejudices, assumptions, and self-concepts influence perceptions and decisions.

   II. To explore the relationship between observation, knowledge, and inference.

   III. To help participants become aware of their personal preconceptions and biases.

Group Size

   Unlimited.

Time Required

   Approximately one and one-half hours.

Materials

   I. One copy of the Sherlock Process Sheet for each participant.

   II. One copy each of the Sherlock Room Description Sheet and the Sherlock Room Diagram for each participant.

   III. One copy each of the Sherlock Inference Sheets I, II, and III for each participant.

   IV. Blank paper and a pencil for each participant.

   V. Newsprint and a felt-tipped marker.

Physical Setting

   A room with chairs and writing surfaces for the participants.

Process

   I. The facilitator introduces the activity by distributing the Sherlock Process Sheet to the participants and reviewing it with them.

II. He then gives each participant a Sherlock Room Description Sheet, a Sherlock Room Diagram, one copy each of the Sherlock Inference Sheets I, II, and III, a blank piece of paper, and a pencil. He tells the participants to read the room description and study the diagram carefully and then to complete the Sherlock Inference Sheets in sequence by following the instructions provided. He allows thirty minutes for them to complete these tasks.

III. While participants are working, the facilitator is available to answer questions. He may advise participants periodically of the time remaining.

IV. The facilitator divides the participants into subgroups of five or six members each and directs them to compare their observations and inferences. (Twenty minutes.)

V. The entire group is reassembled, and the facilitator initiates a discussion in one or more of the following ways:

1. Individuals are selected to summarize their profiles for the group.
2. Each participant is called on to indicate a major observation and inference, while the facilitator lists these on newsprint.
3. Each participant gives a one-word or one-sentence description of the president, and these are listed on newsprint.

Consistencies and inconsistencies are noted and discussed.

VI. The facilitator leads the group in a discussion of the learnings gained from the experience. The following discussion points may be included:

1. Whether we must know to see or see to know.
2. How our prejudices, assumptions, and self-concept affect our observations and decisions.
3. The impressions we can gain about a person we have never met by the nature of his surroundings.
4. The methods we use to integrate inconsistencies in our observations of others.
5. The major influence minor factors can have on us because of preconceptions.
6. How we sense the "whole" from observing parts and how we sense the "parts" from knowing the whole.
7. The observation/knowledge/inference relationship.
8. The difficulty of attaining objectivity in our perceptions of and relationships with others.

The facilitator elicits comments from the participants on personal perceptions and biases they have discovered in themselves as a result of the experience.

Structured Experience 213

Variations

I. The participants can be instructed to complete the Sherlock Inference Sheet in dyads.

II. In step IV, subgroups can be instructed to produce a composite profile of the president of the company.

III. The room description can be rewritten to suit the participants.

IV. The room description can be shortened.

V. The facilitator can project a photo slide of an actual room instead of passing out a diagram.

Similar Structured Experiences: *Vol. III:* Structured Experience **50**; *'72 Annual:* **77**; *'75 Annual:* **137, 142.**

Lecturette Sources: *'72 Annual:* "Communication Modes: An Experiential Lecture"; *'74 Annual:* "Figure/Ground"; *'75 Annual:* "Nonverbal Communication and the Intercultural Encounter."

Notes on the Use of "Sherlock":

Based on material submitted by Rick Roskin.

SHERLOCK PROCESS SHEET

Most people filter their observations of the world through their own self-concepts, biases, prejudices, and knowledge gained from personal experiences. In order to make accurate inferences, we need to understand ourselves as well as the process of relating observation, knowledge, and our "fits of intuition" or inferences based on the first two elements. A. G. Athos and R. E. Coffey, in *Behavior in Organizations: A Multidimensional View* (Englewood Cliffs, New Jersey: Prentice-Hall, 1968), discuss this relationship, which they call "the Sherlock process":

> In order to help you experience the process of sensing the entirety of organizations, we would like you to play Sherlock Holmes with us. As you know, Conan Doyle's masterful detective's genius at observing and reasoning enabled him to solve many baffling mysteries . . . like Sherlock, we will pay careful attention to the process of relating (1) observation, (2) knowledge, and (3) induction and deduction (inference). By observation, we mean, what you see; by knowledge, what meanings, information, and facts you have available to draw upon; by *deduction*, that mental process by which you reason from the general to the specific (All human beings breathe; this man is a living being; therefore this man breathes); and by *induction*, the mental process of reasoning from the specific to the general. (Every dog I have ever seen wags its tail when happy; therefore all dogs wag their tails when happy.)[1]

---

[1] Reprinted by permission of Prentice-Hall, Inc., Englewood Cliffs, New Jersey.

Structured Experience 213

SHERLOCK ROOM DESCRIPTION SHEET

You have just arrived at the ABC company for a job interview. This job sounds like just what you have been looking for; your title would be executive assistant. You would be working directly for the president of the company, who has requested an interview with you. You arrived on time and were met by the president's secretary, who apologized and said that there would be a delay. The president was called unexpectedly into an important conference and will be there for at least fifteen minutes more. In the meantime, the secretary has informed you that you are welcome to wait in the president's private office.

You enter the private office. You know that you will be alone here for at least fifteen minutes. You look around the room, naturally curious about the person you may be working for . . .

The president's office is carpeted in a short shag in blending colors of olive green, brown, and orange. You sit in one of the two orange club chairs to the left of the doorway. Between the chairs is a low wooden table on which there is an empty green glass ashtray. Next to the ashtray are two books of matches; one is from a Playboy Club and the other is from a local restaurant. On the wall behind you is a picture of an old sailing ship in blues and browns. A rubber plant set in a brown and green woven basket sits against the side wall next to the other chair.

Across from where you are sitting is a large wooden desk, with a black leather desk chair. A framed advertisement for the company hangs on the wall behind the desk, and below that sits a closed briefcase. The black waste basket next to the wall by the desk chair is full of papers.

You can see most of the objects on the desk. A matching pen-and-pencil stand and a letter opener sit at the front of the desk. To one side of them is a calculator, and next to that is a brass desk lamp. In front of the lamp is a double metal photograph frame with photographs in it. One is of an attractive woman in her thirties with a young boy about eight years old. The other photograph is of a Dalmation dog in a grassy field. In front of the frame is a stack of green file folders. On the desk in front of the desk chair are a few sheets of paper and a felt-tipped pen.

On the other side of the desk is a yellow stoneware mug. In front of it are a leather tabbed book and a legal-sized yellow pad. The book looks as if it is either an address book or an appointment calendar. Beside the yellow pad lies a pile of unopened mail—envelopes of many sizes. And partially on top of the pile and in back of it are half-folded newspapers: the *Wall Street Journal* and the *New York Times*.

Behind the desk and to one side is a credenza on which seven books are lined up. They are *Roget's Thesaurus*, the *Random House Dictionary*, *Basic Principles of Management*, *Marketing for Today*, *Intergroup and Minority Relations*, *People at Work*, *You Are What You Eat*, and the last year's *World Almanac*. On the far end of the credenza sits a bronze statue; it appears to be of a man sitting with his legs folded in a Yoga position, but it is slightly abstract. In the corner next to the credenza is a philodendron sitting in a brown basket.

There is a window on the far wall, and you get up and go over to look out. Directly in front of the window is a sofa covered in an orange, olive green, and beige print. Two woven throw pillows in brown and beige lie against the arms of the sofa. The draperies at the window behind the sofa are a light beige woven material with an olive green stripe. The view from the window is pleasant: a few tidy shops bordering a small park.

Your gaze turns to the square wooden table next to the sofa. Magazines are scattered in front of a brown ceramic lamp with a beige shade. The magazines are varied: two recent editions of *Time*, and one copy each of *Sports Illustrated*, *The New Yorker*, *Psychology Today*, and *Ebony*. Next to the table is the philodendron.

As you turn to walk back to your chair, you notice that the papers on the desk in front of the chair are your resume and that your statement of your sex has been circled with the felt-tipped pen. Since the president may return at any moment, you sit in the orange chair to wait.

SHERLOCK ROOM DIAGRAM

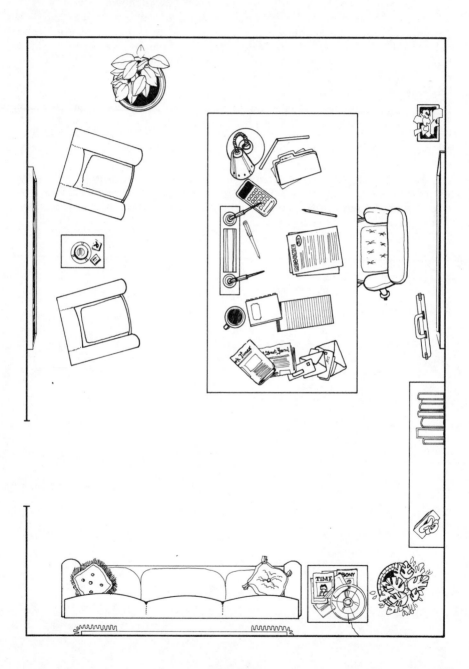

SHERLOCK INFERENCE SHEET I

Read the Sherlock Room Description Sheet and study the room diagram carefully. Then complete the Sherlock Inference Sheet I as follows:
1. In the left-hand column (Observation) note data from your reading that you think are important clues about the kind of person who occupies the room.
2. In the middle column (Knowledge) note any experiences that you may have had that influence your observation.
3. In the right-hand column (Inference) note whatever conclusions you reach as a result of your observations.

OBSERVATION	KNOWLEDGE	INFERENCE
Raw Data	Experiences that Influence Your Observation	Resultant Perception

SHERLOCK INFERENCE SHEET II

Most inferences we make about a situation seem to tie together, to make sense. However, if we examine them carefully, there are often some that do not seem to "fit the picture." In forming conclusions, it is necessary to identify these aspects. They may indicate that the situation is not as obvious as it seems or that we are on the wrong track, or they may merely be inconsistencies—some of which may be explained later and some of which just happen to exist.

On this sheet, list the consistent inferences you have made in one column and the inconsistent ones in the second column.

CONSISTENT

INCONSISTENT

SHERLOCK INFERENCE SHEET III

Using your Sherlock Inference Sheets I and II as bases, write a profile or analysis of the president of the company.

Briefly answer the following questions:

1. Would you accept the job if it were offered to you?

2. How confident are you that you would or would not enjoy working for this person?

3. What do you think would be your degree of satisfaction with this job?

4. How do you think you would be treated by your boss? What type of relationship would you have with the president (would it be formal or informal, cold and distant or friendly; would this person be a colleague, a parent figure, or an authority figure? How would your boss view you?

Structured Experience 213

214. ROLES IMPACT FEELINGS: A ROLE PLAY

Goals

I. To enable participants to become aware of some of the roles they play.

II. To discover how roles produce feelings.

Group Size

A minimum of eight participants. (Can be done with a large group.)

Time Required

Approximately two and one-half hours.

Materials

I. Newsprint and a felt-tipped marker.

II. Two blank name tags for each participant.

III. Blank pieces of paper and a pencil for each participant.

Physical Setting

A room in which the participants can move about freely.

Process

I. The facilitator invites the participants to join in a role play. He does *not* reveal the goals of the experience. The facilitator says that he is going to describe pairs of extreme roles that people play and that each set of roles will demonstrate polarities. He says that the participants will nonverbally play each role for about three minutes after it is described.

II. The facilitator distributes blank paper and pencils to the participants.

III. The facilitator lists the roles on newsprint, one at a time. After listing *each* role, he:

1. Announces the role to be played and explains it briefly.
2. Encourages the participants to "get into" the role nonverbally.

3. Allows about three minutes for the nonverbal activity, depending on how well the group members are responding.
4. Asks the participants (when they are deeply involved in the activity) to become aware of their feelings "right now" and allows about thirty seconds for them to do this.
5. Instructs the participants to record their feelings and how they experienced the particular role. (Two to three minutes.)

The facilitator adds each role in succession to the list on the newsprint as he goes through the activity.

LIST OF ROLES[1]

A. **Bully** (exaggerates aggression, threatens others: "Watch it, Buster.") ←————→ B. **Nice Guy** (exaggerates warmth, tries to please others, smiles: "Oh, what a beautiful day.")

C. **Judge** (exaggerates criticism, mistrusts others, blames: "I know better.") ←————→ D. **Protector** (exaggerates support, spoils others, gives charity: "Let me help you.")

E. **Weakling** (exaggerates sensitivity, helpless, confused, passive: "Please don't hurt me.") ←————→ F. **Dictator** (exaggerates strength, paternalistic and authoritarian, commands: "Do this; don't do that.")

G. **Clinging Vine:** (exaggerates dependency, wants to be taken care of, led by others: "I can't live without you.") ←————→ H. **Calculator** (exaggerates control, perfectionistic, tries to outwit others: "This isn't quite right.")

IV. After the last role play, the facilitator directs the participants to reflect on the following process questions and then to record their answers (ten minutes):
1. Which roles did you identify with most easily?
2. Which roles were the hardest for you to "get into"?
3. Which role did you enjoy most (which was your favorite)?
4. Which role did you either dislike the most or feel to be the most distant from you?

---

[1]Adapted from *Man, the Manipulator* by Everett Shostrom, © 1967 by Abdingdon Press. By permission.

Structured Experience 214

V. The facilitator distributes blank name tags to the participants. He says that each of them is to write his favorite role on his name tag, put the tag on his chest, and then nonverbally portray his favorite role. (Five to ten minutes.)

VI. The facilitator stops the role play and directs the participants to record their feelings about and reactions to the experience. (Three to five minutes.)

VII. The facilitator displays the list of roles on newsprint, noting that the roles across from each other are opposites. He explains that the presupposition[2] is that we do not use the role that is the opposite of our favorite role. He again distributes blank name tags and directs each participant to write on the name tag the role that is the *opposite* of his favorite role.

VIII. Participants nonverbally role play the roles opposite their favorite roles. (Five to fifteen minutes; since these roles are unfamiliar to the participants, it may take some time for them to "get into" the roles and really experience them.)

IX. Participants are instructed to record their feelings about and experiences of the role play. (Three to five minutes.)

X. The facilitator directs the participants to reflect on and then to record their reactions to the entire experience. He encourages them to be aware of how they produced feelings in themselves as they played each role. (Five minutes.)

XI. The group processes the experience. The facilitator may note on newsprint any salient points. He also may focus on how the roles demand "partners" in order to be played out; i.e., the "weakling" is the victim of the "dictator," the "judge" must have someone to judge, etc.

Variations

I. The activity can be stopped after step IV.

II. Other roles can be played, including "positive" ones.

III. A feedback step can be added, during which participants tell how they see each other in terms of the roles they have played.

IV. Participants can be instructed to remain in their favorite or opposite roles while performing some task.

V. In step V, participants can be instructed to make notes on their favorite role and to depict it graphically.

---

[2]See footnote 1.

VI. The experience can be combined with a lecturette on characteristics of the self-actualizing person.

Similar Structured Experiences: *Vol. II:* Structured Experience **28;** *'75 Annual:* **138;** *'76 Annual:* **174;** *Vol. VI:* **203.**

Suggested Instruments: *'76 Annual:* "Inventory of Self-Actualizing Characteristics (ISAC)."

Lecturette Sources: *'72 Annual:* "The Maslow Need Hierarchy"; *'76 Annual:* "Role Functions in a Group."

Notes on the Use of "Roles Impact Feelings":

Submitted by Maury Smith.

Structured Experience 214

215. WHO GETS HIRED?: A MALE/FEMALE ROLE PLAY

Goals

I. To clarify one's personal values regarding sex discrimination.

II. To examine the values held in common on this subject within a group.

III. To explore whether groups of different sexual composition have differences in such values.

IV. To study the way in which such issues are resolved within a group.

V. To gain insight into the subtle aspects of discrimination.

Group Size

Twelve or more participants, with a minimum of six men and six women.

Time Required

One to one and one-half hours.

Materials

A copy of the Who Gets Hired? Background Sheet for each participant.

Physical Setting

A room large enough for all participants and two separate rooms in which the smaller groups can meet without interrupting each other.

Process

I. The facilitator introduces the activity and distributes a copy of the Who Gets Hired? Background Sheet to each participant.

II. Two participants are selected to play Mary Richards and Bill Cook. Each role player goes to another room to consider his or her part.

III. The facilitator discusses the background information with the group, allowing the members to determine which facts are relevant and which are not. He then selects two groups to role play the decision panel, which must decide between the two applicants. One group has two men and three women members while the other group has two women and three men.

IV. The applicants are called in and the decision panels interview both applicants for approximately ten minutes each (in front of all participants). The questions asked are totally at the discretion of the panel members.

V. On completion of the interviews, the two panels leave the group, each going to a separate room. They are told that they will have fifteen minutes in which to make their decisions.

VI. While the panels are absent, the facilitator asks the remaining participants about their reactions in order to determine the personal values of the larger group. At the end of this question period a vote is taken to determine which of the two applicants the group feels should be selected. The facilitator checks to determine if there is a pattern of sexual bias in both the discussion and voting.

VII. The panels return and give their decisions and the reasons for these decisions. Any group discussions are noted. The larger group then asks questions of the two panels to determine how their decisions were made.

VIII. The facilitator leads a discussion of the decision-making processes, pointing out where personal values have intruded and how these values relate to discrimination in employment. He may wish to note the following issues:

1. Male versus female
2. Conventional versus unconventional
3. Educational background
4. Length of work experience
5. Career aspiration, i.e., long term (Mary) versus stepping stone (Bill)
6. Possible effects of the decision on the work group.

Variations

I. Two observers (one male and one female) can be assigned to each panel. They can report their perceptions of the way in which the panels' decisions were made.

II. A time limit of fifteen minutes can be used to examine the influence of a time constraint on decision making. The panels can be told that if a consensus has not been reached a binding vote will be taken. Without the

Structured Experience 215

knowledge of the panels, observers can be asked to note the effect of this constraint.

III. The composition of the principal players can be altered to make one a member of a nonwhite minority group.

IV. The facilitator can acquaint the larger group with the background information; he slowly relates the situation to the group and suggests that they take notes. This is a useful experience in perception; since participants do not have time to note the scenario in full, they will note what they perceive as most important. The variations in perception are interesting and useful for discussion purposes.

V. One discrepant "fact" can be added to each biography, e.g., Mary takes care of her sick mother; Bill smokes marijuana.

Similar Structured Experiences: *Vol. III:* Structured Experiences **62, 63;** *'73 Annual:* **95;** *'76 Annual:* **184.**

Suggested Instrument: *'77 Annual:* "Bem Sex-Role Inventory (BSRI)."

Lecturette Sources: *'73 Annual:* "Confrontation: Types, Conditions, and Outcomes"; *'77 Annual:* "Toward Androgynous Trainers."

Notes on the Use of "Who Gets Hired?":

Submitted by L. V. Entrekin and G. N. Soutar.

WHO GETS HIRED? BACKGROUND SHEET

A medium-sized manufacturing company located in a medium-sized city is looking for a supervisor to oversee a typing pool consisting of thirty female employees and a private secretary. The function of the department is to type all accounting, financial, production, and sales documents for the firm.

The current supervisor, who has been in the job for two years, has been promoted, creating the vacancy. He has practical accounting experience and an associate degree in personnel management from a community college.

It is company policy to promote from within the firm whenever possible. Two employees have applied for the supervisory position, and each knows about the other's application.

Mary Richards is currently the private secretary and "girl Friday" to the outgoing supervisor. Mary is twenty-eight and has been in the department for five years—two as a typist and three in her present position. She is thoroughly familiar with the requirements of the department, is considered a top-notch worker, and is well liked and generally respected.

Mary's life style is considered by some to be unconventional, but it has never interfered with her work. She is unmarried, supports women's liberation, and has said that were she to become pregnant, she would keep the child.

Mary had applied for the position of typing-pool supervisor at the time that the current supervisor was hired. She was told that he was selected over her because of his greater experience and better knowledge of personnel administration. Since then, Mary has completed an associate degree in accounting from the local community college and is taking a course in supervisory skills there.

Mary has told her friends that if she does not get the job this time, she will probably file a discrimination complaint with the regional office of the Equal Employment Opportunity Commission.

Bill Cook is the other applicant for the supervisor's job. He has a bachelor's degree in business administration from the nearby university and is twenty-three years of age. He has worked in the accounting department of the company for eighteen months and has obtained a thorough understanding of company operations. Consequently, his line supervision experience is limited, but he has studied supervision and personnel management in his university program and is considered to have outstanding management potential.

Bill is married and the father of one child. He is a Rotary Club member who coaches Little League baseball. He considers himself to be in the center of the political spectrum and is against abortion. Bill is generally well-thought-of and has demonstrated an ability to get along with people. He sees the supervisor's job as a significant step to a higher managerial position in which he could demonstrate his managerial potential and therefore does not anticipate spending more than two or three years in this position.

Structured Experience 215

216. AFFIRMATION OF TRUST: A FEEDBACK ACTIVITY

Goals

I. To increase understanding of physical, intellectual, and emotional trust.

II. To explore how the trust level existing in the group affects the openness of discussion.

III. To provide an opportunity for group members to give each other feedback on trust.

Group Size

Eight to twelve participants.

Time Required

Approximately two hours.

Materials

I. Eight to twelve slips of paper (or 3" x 5" index cards) for each participant.

II. One Affirmation of Trust Sheet for each participant.

III. A pencil for each participant.

Physical Setting

A room large enough for the activity.

Process

I. The facilitator introduces the activity and outlines the goals.

II. The facilitator says that each member is to take two to three minutes to describe (in a few sentences) to the other members a childhood experience that made a strong impression on him. The facilitator checks to see that everyone has a chance to speak in the time provided. (Twenty-five minutes.)

III. The facilitator then directs the members to discuss the following (twenty minutes):
   1. What kind of situations cause you to be afraid?
   2. What kind of life situation do you wish to have at some time in the future?
   3. What makes you happy?
   4. What do you do best?

IV. The facilitator instructs each member to remove a shoe and to place it alongside the shoes of other members in a designated place, outside the group's meeting area. Each member is to identify his shoe by writing his name on a slip of paper and putting it in front of the shoe.

V. The facilitator distributes slips of paper, a pencil, and an Affirmation of Trust Sheet to each participant. He directs the members to take a few minutes to familiarize themselves with the Affirmation of Trust Sheet.

VI. Each member is then directed to select a maximum of five statements from the Affirmation of Trust Sheet that best describe his trust in another member of the group; to write the other member's name, the numbers of the applicable statements, and his own signature on a slip of paper; and to deposit the slip in the other member's shoe. Each member is instructed to do this for every other member of the group. (Some statements may be duplicated.)

VII. After all members have distributed their slips, each one retrieves his own shoe with the slips left in it. He reads each of the slips directed to him by the other members and records the numbers on his Affirmation of Trust Sheet. (Names of members giving the feedback may also be recorded.)

VIII. Members discuss their reactions to their slips with the group. Participants are encouraged to solicit clarification of their feedback.

IX. The facilitator leads the group in a discussion of the experience, focusing on its goals.

Variations

I. Steps II and III can be omitted.

II. Participants can be instructed to distribute as many of the thirty-five statements as they wish to.

III. The statements can be preprinted on individual strips and given to each participant in packages of thirty-five each.

Structured Experience 216

IV. The statements on the Affirmation of Trust Sheet can be written or adapted to deal with specific issues in the group.

V. Participants can be directed to distribute slips only to persons of their choice.

Similar Structured Experiences: *Vol. III:* Structured Experiences **55, 57;** *'77 Annual:* **196;** *Vol. VI:* **208.**

Suggested Instrument: *'77 Annual:* "TORI Group Self-Diagnosis Scale."

Lecturette Source: *'72 Annual:* "TORI Theory and Practice."

Notes on the Use of "Affirmation of Trust":

_____
Submitted by Brian P. Holleran.

AFFIRMATION OF TRUST SHEET

1. I would trust you to share your happiness with me.
2. I would trust you to hold my money.
3. I would trust you to care for my children.
4. I would hope that you would tell me how others perceive me.
5. I would trust you to help me if I were incapacitated in some way.
6. I would hope that you would give me help if I needed it.
7. I would trust you to keep an appointment with me.
8. I would hope that you would tell me if I sound phony.
9. I would hope that you would share some good fortune with me.
10. I would trust you to be honest with me.
11. I would trust you not to gossip about me in my absence.
12. I would trust you to keep secret any disclosure of some intimacy I shared with you.
13. I would trust you enough to tell you about those I love.
14. I would trust that you would be an excellent traveling companion for a trip abroad.
15. I would trust you to be executor of my estate.
16. I would trust you to drive my car.
17. I would trust you to pay back any money I might loan you.
18. I would trust you to live in and take care of my apartment/house in my absence.
19. I would trust you to complete any task I might give you.
20. I would hope that you would give me a place to sleep if I needed it.
21. I would hope that you would freely give me your friendship.
22. I would hope that you would offer me emotional support when I needed it.
23. I would seek your advice on interpersonal relationships.
24. I would hope that you would share some of your free time with me.
25. I would share my creations with you.
26. I would trust you with my life.
27. I would hope to be comfortable with you without having to talk.
28. I would trust that what you say is based on fact and not fabrication.
29. I would trust you to allow me to vent my anger about other persons or events.
30. I would trust your views about political matters.
31. I would hope that you would express the degree of affection you have for me.
32. I would trust you enough to share my feelings toward you.
33. I would trust you enough to share some of my sexual intimacies with you.
34. I would trust you to fix me up with a blind date.
35. I would trust you to represent me astutely in business affairs.

217. NEGOTIATING DIFFERENCES: AVOIDING POLARIZATION

Goals

I. To identify the dimensions along which people may differ.

II. To explore the potential for persons to complement as well as conflict with each other, as a result of such differences.

III. To negotiate a contract for coordinating different personal styles or opinions.

Group Size

An unlimited number of triads.

Time Required

Approximately one hour.

Materials

Newsprint and a felt-tipped marker.

Physical Setting

A room large enough for triads to interact without disrupting each other.

Process

I. The facilitator elicits from participants a list of polar dimensions used to describe people (e.g., assertive/unassertive, task/social, cognitive/ affective, etc.) and posts it on newsprint.

II. The facilitator identifies a dimension that is of interest to participants and on which participants appear well distributed. He instructs the participants to form a "line-up," with the ends of the line representing the poles of the dimension and the participants distributed along it according to their perceptions of themselves.

III. The persons at one end of the line are told to form a pair with a person at the opposite end. The one-third of the participants who are closest to the "middle-of-the-road" position are assigned to serve as observers of the polar pairs and are each to help keep their partner pair on the task.

IV. The triads (two opposite participants and their process observer) disperse around the room.

V. Each opposite in a pair describes himself to his partner regarding his pole of the dimension.

VI. Each partner then states his stereotype of his partner on that dimension.

VII. The partners discuss how their differences complement each other and then discuss how their differences potentially conflict.

VIII. The pair finally negotiates a contract in which they attempt to complement each other and prevent conflict or deal with conflict constructively when it occurs.

IX. The process observer for each pair shares his perceptions of their negotiation process.

X. The entire group is reconvened, and the facilitator leads a discussion of the process. He may focus on such issues as methods of confrontation, win-lose situations, or styles of resolving conflict.

Variations

I. The activity can be repeated with different dimensions being discussed.

II. The experience can be used as an intervention in a polarized situation with the line-up focusing on an actual issue.

III. In step VI, partners can take turns paraphrasing what the other has said, rather than sharing stereotypes.

IV. The third person can serve as an intervener instead of as an observer.

V. Participants can line up in categories (strongly disagree, disagree, agree, strongly agree), depicting the way they feel about a particular issue. They are then paired off ("strongly disagree" with "strongly agree," "disagree" with "agree," etc.). No middle-ground (uncommitted, neutral) positions are allowed.

Similar Structured Experiences: *Vol. I:* Structured Experience 8; *Vol. III:* **57, 59, 62;** *'73 Annual:* **97;** *Vol. IV:* **116;** *Vol. V:* **169;** *'76 Annual:* **183.**

Lecturette Sources: *'73 Annual:* "Win/Lose Situations," "Risk-Taking," "Confrontation: Types, Conditions, and Outcomes"; *'76 Annual:* "Clarity of Expression in Interpersonal Communication"; *'77 Annual:* "Constructive Conflict in Discussions: Learning to Manage Disagreements Effectively."

Structured Experience 217

Notes on the Use of "Negotiating Differences":

Submitted by David X. Swenson.

218. SPY: AN INTERGROUP ACTIVITY

Goals

    I. To explore the impact of competition between groups.

    II. To demonstrate different methods of group problem solving.

    III. To examine the dynamics of suspicion and distrust in a group.

    IV. To observe the process of a leaderless group in the completion of a specific task.

Group Size

    A minimum of two groups with six to ten participants each (groups should be of equal size).

Time Required

    Approximately one and one-half hours.

Materials

    I. One set of fourteen blocks for each group and another set from which the facilitator constructs the model (see Directions for Making a Spy Model).

    II. A Spy Team Design Instruction Sheet for each participant.

    III. An envelope containing Spy Special Instructions for each participant. (On each sheet, the facilitator is to mark an "x," *by hand*, in the block next to the words "You are not a spy.")

    IV. Two Spy Team Design Work Sheets for each group.

    V. A watch for each timekeeper.

    VI. A copy of the Spy Timekeeper Sheet for each timekeeper.

    VII. A copy of the Spy Observer Sheet for each observer.

    VIII. Pencils for each observer, timekeeper, and group.

    IX. Newsprint and a felt-tipped marker.

Physical Setting

Two rooms, or one room with a small partitioned-off area for placement of the model. One room should be large enough for each group to work at a separate table. The model is placed on a table in the second room or partitioned area.

Process

I. The facilitator forms equal groups of six to ten members each. He obtains volunteers to function as observers and timekeepers (one of each for each group). He then assigns each group to a work table.

II. A set of blocks is apportioned to each team. A Spy Team Design Instruction Sheet and an envelope containing Spy Special Instructions are given to each participant. A watch, a Spy Timekeeper Sheet, and a pencil are given to each timekeeper. A Spy Observer Sheet and a pencil are handed to each observer; and two Spy Team Design Work Sheets and a pencil are given to each team.

III. The facilitator goes over the Spy Team Design Instruction Sheet with the members. He informs them that:
1. Each team will have to decide whether or not to use all fourteen blocks.
2. There may be one or more spies in a group.
3. Members may write on the work sheets, but may *not* take the work sheets with them when they view the model.
4. Teams may arrange their blocks in order, so long as no two blocks are touching.

IV. The facilitator briefs the timekeepers and observers; he goes over their instruction sheets with them. (He does *not* tell the observers that there are no spies.)

V. The facilitator informs the groups of the location of the model and gives the signal to begin the activity.

VI. When one hour has passed, the facilitator calls time. The timekeepers for each group give their reports, and the facilitator records the scores on newsprint. Then the observer from each group makes his report. The facilitator leads a discussion of the following group processes: the impact of competition between groups; methods of group problem solving; and the interaction between members of a leaderless group. He may relate these to time scores and the productivity of the groups.

VII. The facilitator divulges the fact that there were *no* spies in any group, and the total group discusses the behavior surrounding this issue. The group members can also discuss any feelings they may have experienced about being misled on this point.

VIII. Finally the facilitator discusses the learnings gained from the experience and their application to real-life situations.

Variations

I. To increase competition between groups, a small amount of money can be collected from each participant as a prize for the winning team.

II. To examine intergroup dynamics, one essential block from each group can be given to another group.

III. To assist groups, one or more correct numbers may be written in advance on each work sheet.

IV. To aid in timing the competition segment, a sixty-minute cassette tape can be made with the "time remaining" announced at fifteen-minute intervals for forty-five minutes, five-minute intervals for the next ten minutes, one-minute intervals for the next four minutes, and fifteen-second intervals for the last minute.

V. Different materials can be used.

VI. Planning minutes can "cost" one point each and assembly minutes three points each in order to determine a winning team.

Similar Structured Experiences: *Vol. II:* Structured Experiences **32, 35;** *Vol. III:* **54, 61;** *'72 Annual:* **81;** *Vol. IV:* **105;** *Vol. V:* **160, 161;** *'77 Annual:* **194.**

Lecturette Sources: *'72 Annual:* "McGregor's Theory X-Theory Y Model"; *'73 Annual:* "Win/ Lose Situations"; *'76 Annual:* "Role Functions in a Group."

Notes on the Use of "Spy":

Submitted by Stephen J. Schoen.

Structured Experience 218

DIRECTIONS FOR MAKING A SPY MODEL

Each group receives a set of fourteen blocks. Twelve of the blocks are needed to duplicate the model.

The blocks can be made out of 2″ x 2″ wooden cubes. The top and bottom of each block are blank; the sides are painted with the figures specified below:

Block	Figures			
	Side 1	Side 2	Side 3	Side 4
1	5	0	8	7
2	7	+	1	−
3*	7	+	1	−
4	7	6	4	=
5	1	9	0	3
6	1	4	8	6
7	5	−	+	0
8	8	9	2	=
9	4	2	+	5
10*	2	3	9	7
11	8	3	2	0
12	+	6	=	−
13	9	4	1	=
14	9	4	1	=

*Block not needed to construct model.

With an additional set of blocks, the facilitator constructs a model to be viewed by the teams. He does this by arranging blocks as shown in the following two views:

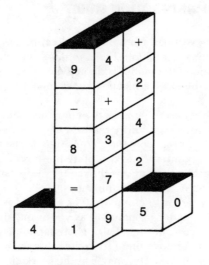

Model View #1

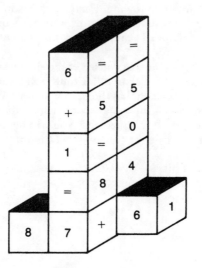

Model View #2

Structured Experience 218

SPY TEAM DESIGN INSTRUCTION SHEET

On the table (in the next room) is a model made of blocks. On each of the four sides of a block there is either a number, a minus sign, a plus sign, or an equal sign. The general shape of the model is depicted on the Spy Team Design Work Sheet. The tops of the blocks are blacked out since only the sides of each block are marked.

Take the blocks allotted to your team and spread them out on the table so that no two blocks are touching. Verify that you have fourteen blocks.

The task of each team is to construct a duplicate of the model in the shortest time. You will have sixty minutes to complete the task. The duplicate must be "exact"; the shape must be the same as the model, and all numbers, plus, minus, and equal signs must be in the correct positions.

The activity is divided into two parts. The first part is preparation. Take as much of the sixty minutes for preparation as you want, since preparation time will not count in the competition. During preparation, you may handle the blocks, but you may not remove them from the table or place them so that they are touching any other blocks. You may use the work sheets, but you may not remove them from the table.

Any team member (one at a time only) may go to view the model but may look at it from one side of the table only. He may look at the model for as long as he wishes and may return as often as he wishes, but he is not permitted to see all sides of the model in any one viewing. Each time a team member goes to view the model, regardless of how long he remains, fifteen seconds will be charged to your team's construction time. Team members may view the model at any time during preparation or construction.

When your team feels ready to construct the model, notify the timekeeper and begin constructing. Your construction time will automatically start if two blocks are deliberately placed so that they are touching. When you believe that your model is correct, notify the timekeeper, who will stop the timing. Your model will then be checked. If it is incorrect, you will be told that there is at least one mistake, and your construction time will continue.

SPY SPECIAL INSTRUCTIONS

(For your eyes only . . .)

In real life, all team members do not always work for the same goals. Sometimes people do things to reach personal rather than team goals. They may work against team goals because of group friction, lack of trust, inability to get along with a supervisor, etc. There *may* be such a person in your group. We will call that person a "spy." It is possible that more than one spy may be in a group.

If you are a spy, you are to do everything in your power to hinder the efforts of your team, without letting anyone know that you are a spy.

If a team member thinks that another member is a spy, he can accuse that person of spying. The rest of the team will vote, and if there is unanimous agreement, the spy can be excluded from any further deliberations of the group.

☐ You are a spy.

☐ You are *not* a spy.

SPY TEAM DESIGN WORK SHEET

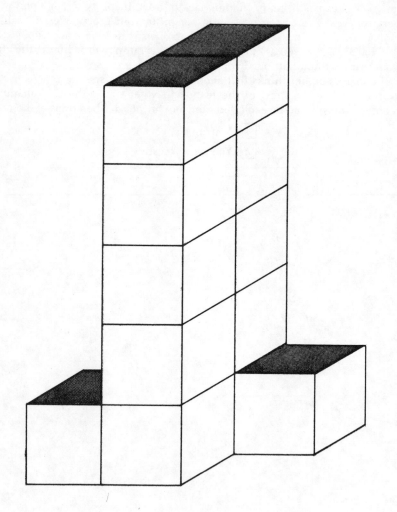

SPY TIMEKEEPER SHEET

You are to make an accurate record of the time used by your team. It is important that the time be accurate.

In the space marked "visits to model," place a check mark *each* time a member from the team you are observing goes to view the model.

Do not time anything until the team tells you it is ready to start constructing the model. As soon as it tells you, start keeping time.

When the team tells you that it has completed the task, calculate the elapsed time and ask the facilitator to check the model. If the model is incorrect, continue keeping time until the team again tells you it has completed the task, then calculate the elapsed time again and ask the facilitator to check the model.

At the end of the activity, add up the check marks in item 1 and multiply by fifteen seconds. Then write down in item 2 the actual time used according to the watch. Last, add items 1 and 2 to get a total construction time for item 3.

1. Visits to model: _____ x fifteen seconds = _____ min. _____ sec.

2. Construction time: _____ min. _____ sec.

3. Total construction time (item 1 plus item 2)   = _____ min. _____ sec.

SPY OBSERVER SHEET

You are to observe one team during the activity. Feel free to wander around the team as much as you like, but do not speak and do not answer any questions. Below is a list of things you should be looking for. Take notes and be prepared to discuss your observations after the activity.

Did any one member emerge as a leader?

Did other group roles emerge, such as tension reliever, organizer, etc.?

Was there friction in the group? Why?

Did people wonder who the spy was?

How was the preparation time used?

How was the construction time used?

Describe the level of teamwork you observed:

Who were high participators? Low participators?

Any other observations:

219. ESCALATION: AN ASSERTION ACTIVITY

Goals

I. To allow participants to experience success in communicating while under stress.

II. To enable participants to practice communicating effectively in stressful situations.

Group Size

Any number of groups of six or eight participants each.

Time Required

One to two hours.

Materials

A pencil and paper for each participant.

Physical Setting

A room large enough so that each group can work without being disturbed by other groups.

Process

I. The facilitator introduces the experience and outlines its goals.

II. He leads the participants in brainstorming a list of typical stressful situations. (Approximately ten minutes.)

III. The facilitator gives a lecturette defining assertion and presents some specific guidelines for formulating an assertive response.

IV. The facilitator distributes pencils and paper and says that each participant is to record a hypothetical or actual stressful situation that he would like to practice responding to. He says that each participant should also write down an assertive response that he would like to be able to make in the situation that he has described. (Ten minutes.)

V. Participants are directed to choose partners and to share with their partners what each has written.

VI. The dyads are directed to form groups of four to six participants each.

VII. The facilitator says that one participant from each group is to volunteer to share his situation and desired response with the members of his group.

VIII. The facilitator directs the members of each group other than the volunteer and his partner to stand in a line. He explains that these people will serve as "hasslers" to create a stressful situation. The person on the left is designated the "mild hassler," and the roles are escalated from left to right so that the member on the right will serve as the most intense "hassler."

IX. The facilitator then explains the roles (volunteer, partner, and hasslers) to be played by the group members:

1. The volunteer is to describe the stressful situation that he has written about. He then is to respond to each hassler, in turn, with the assertive response that he has stated he would like to be able to make.

2. The volunteer's partner is to be sure that he understands the situation and response and is to offer suggestions for making the response as specific and assertive as possible. He accompanies the volunteer as he proceeds from one hassler to the next. He (a) makes sure that the hasslers follow their role guidelines; (b) lends support, by his presence, to the volunteer; (c) solicits *positive* feedback from the group members on the volunteer's performance after each new hassler has been dealt with; and (d) confers with the volunteer, following each solicitation of feedback, on one or two things the volunteer would like to do or could do to improve his response to the next hassler.

3. Each hassler is to play the role of antagonist in the situation described by the volunteer and is to remain true to that situation without expanding or adapting it. Each hassler is to play his role with the degree of intensity assigned to it; "mild" hasslers may ask one question or make one statement, and so on. (Hasslers in the far right position are cautioned not to hassle indefinitely.) Finally, *all hasslers are to ensure a successful experience for the volunteer by allowing the volunteer to "win" each encounter as he progresses along the line of hasslers.*

X. The role play is conducted. (Approximately twenty minutes.)

XI. The members of each group discuss the activity in terms of what helped and what hindered the volunteer in making an effective assertive response and the degree to which the experience brought about an increase in his confidence and skill in communicating the response.

XII. The total group reassembles, and subgroups report on their discussions. The facilitator then leads the total group in processing the experience.

XIII. Steps X through XII are repeated with other volunteers as time allows.

Variations

I. "Canned" situations can be used instead of ones brainstormed by the group members.

II. The activity can be performed by one group initially, to serve as a demonstration for the total group. It can then be performed by many groups simultaneously.

Similar Structured Experience: *Vol. VI:* Structured Experience **206.**

Lecturette Sources: *'73 Annual:* "Confrontation: Types, Conditions, and Outcomes"; *'76 Annual:* "Dealing with Anger," "Assertion Theory."

Notes on the Use of "Escalation":

Submitted by Colleen Kelley. The techniques of escalation and the use of a hierarchy are common in behavior therapy, especially in assertion training. See, for example, Rimm and Masters (*Behavior Therapy: Techniques and Empirical Findings*, New York: Academic Press, 1974, pp. 99-103) and Lange and Jakubowski (*Responsible Assertive Behavior: Cognitive/Behavioral Procedures for Trainers*, Champaign, Ill.: Research Press, 1976, pp. 108-111). See also C. Kelley, "Assertion: The Literature Since 1970" in *The 1977 Annual*.

220. DYADIC RISK TAKING: A PERCEPTION CHECK

Goals

I. To experience the feelings associated with mild risk-taking behavior.

II. To experiment with controlling the level of risk one is willing to take.

III. To experience specific feedback on the degree to which another perceives one's risk.

Group Size

Any number of dyads.

Time Required

Approximately one hour.

Materials

A Dyadic Risk Taking Score Sheet and a pencil for each participant.

Physical Setting

A room that can be divided into working areas in which the dyads can confer in relative privacy; a chair for each member.

Process

I. The facilitator introduces the concept of self-disclosure as a form of risk behavior and invites the participants to explore their own risk boundaries by exchanging disclosure statements. (The Johari Window concept is useful for explaining disclosure and feedback.)

II. The facilitator explains the experience fully to the participants; he emphasizes that each participant can make "zero-risk" statements if he so chooses. He also makes it clear that this is not a "competition," but rather an opportunity to explore one's own risk boundaries.

III. The facilitator distributes Dyadic Risk Taking Score Sheets and pencils to the participants.

IV. The participants are paired off, and the dyads go to their working areas.

V. The dyadic members sit side by side, facing in opposite directions, i.e., shoulder to shoulder. This position enables them to regulate eye contact and nonverbal involvement as they see fit.

VI. The participants take turns within each dyad making disclosure statements, according to instructions on the Dyadic Risk Taking Score Sheet. Each statement is a statement about the speaker himself, and represents an attempt to disclose significant "risky" information about himself. As the participant makes a disclosure statement, his partner makes a guess as to the relative risk level of the statement—*for the speaker*—and records it in numerical form. The participants take turns through ten independent statements each, total the scores, and exchange them.

VII. Participants are allowed to continue in post-experience discussion as dyads until all dyads are finished. The facilitator then forms small groups of six to eight members each for sharing the experience.

Variations

I. The dyads may be composed of strangers or of people who share significant ongoing relationships such as close friends or mates.

II. In step VII the facilitator can direct the participants to express their reactions to the experience through body movements or other nonverbal means.

III. Each participant might try to guess his "score" before it is divulged by his partner; the partners can then discuss any significant differences between the guess and the actual score.

Similar Structured Experiences: *Vol. I:* Structured Experience 21; *Vol. II:***45;** *Vol. III:* **70;** *Vol. IV:* **116, 123;** *'73 Annual:* **99;** *Vol. V:* **169;** *'76 Annual:* **180;** *'77 Annual:* **190.**

Suggested Instruments: *Vol. IV:* "Risk-Taking Behavior in Groups Questionnaire"; *'74 Annual:* "Self-Disclosure Questionnaire."

Lecturette Sources: *'72 Annual:* "Risk-Taking and Error Protection Styles"; *'73 Annual:* "The Johari Window: A Model for Soliciting and Giving Feedback," "Risk-Taking."

Submitted by Karl G. Albrecht and Walton C. Boshear.

Structured Experience 220

Notes on the Use of "Dyadic Risk Taking":

DYADIC RISK TAKING SCORE SHEET

Instructions: This structured experience enables you to experiment with risk-taking behavior in a supportive environment.

You and your partner are to take turns making statements. Each statement should be a statement about the *speaker* (not about his personal "statistics," hobbies, past experiences, relationships with other people, etc.). The statement should represent an attempt to disclose feelings, emotions, attitudes, ideas, etc., that represent a risk to the speaker.

You are to keep a "point score" for each statement your partner makes. You may also want to record some key words or nonverbal cues from each statement to help you remember what your partner communicated. *Do not reply to your partner's statement*—simply make one of your own. Do not show him his score until after each of you has made a total of ten statements.

Award points for each of the ten statements according to the following:

Scoring Criteria

3 points: I believe he is taking a genuine risk (for him) in telling me this.

2 points: I believe he is taking a mild risk (for him) in telling me this.

1 point:　I believe he is not taking a risk in telling me this.

0 points: I believe he is avoiding risk in telling me this.

	SCORE	KEY WORDS	NONVERBAL CUES
1.	_____	_____	_____
2.	_____	_____	_____
3.	_____	_____	_____
4.	_____	_____	_____
5.	_____	_____	_____
6.	_____	_____	_____
7.	_____	_____	_____
8.	_____	_____	_____
9.	_____	_____	_____
10.	_____	_____	_____
Total	_____	_____	_____

Structured Experience 220

CONTRIBUTORS

Karl G. Albrecht
President
Management Sciences
P.O. Box 99097
San Diego, California 92109
(714) 272-3776

Anthony G. Banet, Jr.
Senior Consultant
University Associates, Inc.
7596 Eads Avenue
La Jolla, California 92037
(714) 454-8821

Jordan P. Berliner
Senior Associate
Drake-Beam & Associates
1001 E. Touhy Avenue
Des Plaines, Illinois 60018
(312) 299-2286

Walton C. Boshear
President
Creative Management
1125 Camino Del Mar
Del Mar, California 92014
(714) 755-2484

Samuel Dolinsky
Training and Employment Specialist
Inmont Corporation
1255 Broad Street
Clifton, New Jersey 07015
(201) 773-8200

L. V. Entrekin
Lecturer in Commerce
The University of Western Australia
Nedlands, Western Australia 6009
802874

Ken Frey
Staff Development Manager
United Co-Operatives of Ontario
3395 Cliff Road North
Mississauga, Ontario, Canada L5A 3M7
(416) 270-3560

Donald L. Garris
Professor
Department of Counseling
Shippensburg State College
Shippensburg, Pennsylvania 17257
(717) 532-7537

Gary R. Gemmill
Associate Professor
  of Organizational Behavior
School of Management
Syracuse University
Syracuse, New York 13210
(315) 423-2601

Brian P. Holleran
Associate Professor
Speech and Theater Department
221 Administration
State University College
Oneonta, New York 13820
(607) 431-3402

J. David Jackson
Organization Development Consultant
Jackson-Smith & Associates
3284 Yonge Street
Toronto, Ontario, Canada
(416) 487-4181

Colleen Kelley
Human Relations Consultant
2500 Torrey Pines Road
La Jolla, California 92037
(714) 453-8165

Clyde E. Lee
Programs Manager
IBM Australia Limited
Bradfield Highway and Kent Street
Sydney, N.S.W., Australia
20531

Donald K. McLeod
Police Training Coordinator
Rockland County Police Training
  Program
Fire Training Center
Fireman Memorial Drive
Pomona, New York 10970

Stephan H. Putnam
Visiting Lecturer in Group Relations
School of Public Health
The University of North Carolina
  at Chapel Hill
Chapel Hill, North Carolina 27514
(919) 966-1058

Neil E. Rand
Organization Development Consultant
Ann Arbor Consulting Associates, Inc.
100 City Center Building
Ann Arbor, Michigan 48108
(313) 995-2404

Rick Roskin
Associate Professor
  of Organizational Behavior
Memorial University of Newfoundland
St. John's, Newfoundland
Canada A1C 5S7

Stephen J. Schoen
Counseling Psychologist
Coordinator, TIGER
Veterans Administration Hospital
Richmond, Virginia 23249

Ernest M. Schuttenberg
Associate Professor
College of Education
The Cleveland State University
Cleveland, Ohio 44115
(216) 687-4612

Evelyn Sieburg
Communication Consultant
Family and Personal Relations Center
1767 Grand Avenue
San Diego, California 92109
(714) 270-6060

Dennie L. Smith
Associate Professor
Department of Curriculum & Instruction
Memphis State University
Memphis, Tennessee 38152
(901) 454-2338

Maury Smith
Director
Alverna Retreat House
8140 Spring Mill Road
Indianapolis, Indiana 46260
(317) 253-7016

G. N. Soutar
Lecturer in Commerce
The University of Western Australia
Nedlands, Western Australia 6009
802909

Mary E. Sparks
Clinical Psychology Intern
Counseling-Psychological Services
  Center
University of Texas at Austin
Austin, Texas 78712
(512) 471-3515

David X. Swenson
Chief Psychologist
Douglas County Mental Health Center
1313 Belknap Street
Superior, Wisconsin 54880
(715) 394-0367

Donald L. Thompson
Employee Training Consultant
Pennsylvania Department
  of Environmental Resources
Bureau of Human Resource Management
Harrisburg, Pennsylvania 17120
(717) 787-1443

Gerald N. Weiskott
Counseling Psychologist
The Ohio State University
Counseling and Consultation Service
1739 North High Street
Columbus, Ohio 43210
(614) 422-5766

Please add the following name to your mailing list.

_____

_____

_____

_____ Zip _____

Primary Organizational Affiliation: ☐ fill in with one
number from below

1. Education
2. Business & Industry
3. Religious Organization
4. Government Agency
5. Counseling

6. Mental Health
7. Community, Voluntary, and/or
   Service Organization
8. Health Care
9. Library
0. Consulting

Please add the following name to your mailing list.

_____

_____

_____

_____ Zip _____

Primary Organizational Affiliation: ☐ fill in with one
number from below

1. Education
2. Business & Industry
3. Religious Organization
4. Government Agency
5. Counseling

6. Mental Health
7. Community, Voluntary, and/or
   Service Organization
8. Health Care
9. Library
0. Consulting